101 IQ Building Word Games

Mayme Allen & Janine Kelsch

Sterling Publishing Co., Inc.
New York

We wish to acknowledge the support and dedicated assistance of Chris Powell in helping us bring *101 IQ Building Word Games* to fruition. At Sterling, we're also deeply grateful to Shelia Anne Barry, for encouraging the development of this book, and to Laurel Ornitz, for her outstanding editorial eye.

Illustrations by Mayme Allen

Library of Congress Cataloging-in-Publication Data Available

10 9 8 7 6 5 4 3 2 1

Published in 2003 by Sterling Publishing Co., Inc.
387 Park Avenue South, New York, NY 10016
©1991 by Mayme Allen & Janine Kelsch
Originally published under the title *101 Word Games*
Distributed in Canada by Sterling Publishing
C/o Canadian Manda Group, One Atlantic Avenue, Suite 105
Toronto, Ontario, Canada M6K 3E7
Distributed in Great Britain by Chrysalis Books
64 Brewery Road, London N7 9NT England
Distributed in Australia by Capricorn Link (Australia) Pty. Ltd.
P.O. Box 704, Windsor, NSW 2756 Australia

Sterling ISBN 1-4027-0953-6

CONTENTS

For Chris, Dave, and Polly

TRICKY TRIOS

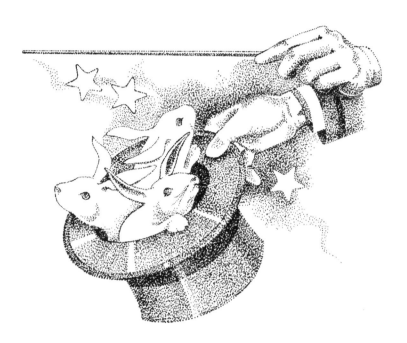

General Instructions

For the games that follow, list as many words as you can, using the designated letters in the sequence specified. You can use only one form of each word—for example, *telegraph* shouldn't also be listed as *telegraphing*. Words with different meanings, however, such as *desert* and *desertion*, can be used, even if they have the same root. No proper nouns allowed in these games.

TRICKY TRIOS #1
"EGR"

The letters "egr" appear in this sequence in at least 25 words—list as many as you can.

_____ _____ _____
_____ _____ _____
_____ _____ _____
_____ _____ _____
_____ _____ _____
_____ _____ _____
_____ _____ _____
_____ _____ _____
_____ _____ _____
_____ _____ _____

TRICKY TRIOS #2
"OXY"

The letters "oxy" appear in this sequence in at least 21 words—list as many as you can.

_____ _____ _____
_____ _____ _____
_____ _____ _____
_____ _____ _____
_____ _____ _____
_____ _____ _____
_____ _____ _____

TRICKY TRIOS #3
"ADI"

The letters "adi" appear in this sequence in at least 90 words—
list as many as you can.

TRICKY TRIOS #4
"ERT"

The letters "ert" appear in this sequence in at least 115 words—list as many as you can.

_____   _____   _____
_____   _____   _____
_____   _____   _____
_____   _____   _____
_____   _____   _____
_____   _____   _____
_____   _____   _____
_____   _____   _____
_____   _____   _____
_____   _____   _____

TRICKY TRIOS #5
"AZI"

The letters "azi" appear in this sequence in at least 19 words—
list as many as you can.

_____   _____   _____
_____   _____   _____
_____   _____   _____
_____   _____   _____
_____   _____   _____
_____   _____   _____
_____   _____   _____

TRICKY TRIOS #6
"OQU"

The letters "oqu" appear in this sequence in at least 16 words—list as many as you can.

_____   _____   _____
_____   _____   _____
_____   _____   _____
_____   _____   _____
_____   _____   _____
_____   _____   _____

TRICKY TRIOS #7
"ICO"

The letters "ico" appear in this sequence in at least 95 words—list as many you can.

_____   _____   _____
_____   _____   _____
_____   _____   _____
_____   _____   _____
_____   _____   _____
_____   _____   _____
_____   _____   _____
_____   _____   _____
_____   _____   _____
_____   _____   _____
_____   _____   _____
_____   _____   _____
_____   _____   _____

TRICKY TRIOS #8
"LPH"

The letters "lph" appear in this sequence in at least 11 words—list as many you can.

TRICKY TRIOS #9
"EME"

The letters "eme" appear in this sequence in at least 63 words—list as many you can.

_____   _____   _____
_____   _____   _____
_____   _____   _____
_____   _____   _____
_____   _____   _____
_____   _____   _____
_____   _____   _____
_____   _____   _____
_____   _____   _____
_____   _____   _____
_____   _____   _____
_____   _____   _____
_____   _____   _____
_____   _____   _____
_____   _____   _____
_____   _____   _____
_____   _____   _____
_____   _____   _____
_____   _____   _____
_____   _____   _____
_____   _____   _____
_____   _____   _____
_____   _____   _____

WORDWORKS

General Instructions

In the games that follow, vocabulary fiends can find many hidden words in the designated word for each game. Use only words of four or more letters and no proper nouns.

WORDWORKS #1
"Gamester"

Find up to 82 words in the playful noun above. A score of 40 deserves a red ribbon; 50, a blue one; and 60, the dictionary hall of fame!

(4 letters)   **(5 letters)**   **(6 letters)**

(7 letters)

WORDWORKS #2
"Favorite"

Find at least 50 words in this shining example. Score 30 to be a tough contender; go for broke with 35; find 45, and you'll be favored in any word race!

(4 letters)   **(5 letters)**

WORDWORKS #3
"Betrothal"

There are 114 words concealed here. Finding 70 means you're a real word lover; 80, you're totally committed; and 90 or more gets the brass ring!

(4 letters)　　　　　　**(5 letters)**　　　　　　**(6 letters)**

(7 letters)

WORDWORKS #4
"Development"

Seek out the 94 words concealed here. Get 60 words for a good foundation; 70, and you've done the framework; 80 or more, and you're a master wordsmith!

(4 letters)

(5 letters)

(6 letters)

(7 letters)

(8 letters)

(9 letters)

WORDWORKS #5
"Exemplary"

Search for the 68 words hidden here. Finding 40 is outstanding; 50 makes you a truly superb player; 55, and you are a paragon of gamesmanship!

(4 letters)   **(5 letters)**   **(6 letters)**

(7 letters)

WORDWORKS #6
"Popularity"

Find at least 100 words in this fun-fest. Come up with 75, and you're hot; nail 85, and you're totally rad; 90 or more, and you're a party animal!

(4 letters)   **(5 letters)**   **(6 letters)**

(7 letters)   **(8 letters)**

WORDWORKS #7
"Historical"

Hidden in this stumper are at least 112 words. Locate 70, and you're a scholar; score 80, and be a professor; discover 90, and you've got tenure!

(4 letters)

(5 letters)

(6 letters)

(7 letters)

(8 letters)

WORDWORKS #8
"Concentration"

At least 150 words can be found in the word above, including one 11-letter word! A total of 75 is good; 90 is excellent; and 110 means your powers of concentration are awesome!

(4 letters)

(5 letters)

(6 letters)

(7 letters)

(8 letters)

(9 letters)

(10 letters)

(11 letters)

WORDWORKS #9
"Xylophone"

This noteworthy number will reveal at least 40 words. Find 25, and you've made the band; 30 hands you the baton; 35, you're Lionel Hampton!

(4 letters)   **(5 letters)**   **(6 letters)**

WORDWORKS #10
"Nasturtium"

As you tiptoe through the hothouse, look for at least 84 new words. Uncover 55, and you've got a green thumb; find 65, you're president of the garden club; cultivate 75, and you are a wordiculturist!

(4 letters)

(5 letters)

(6 letters)

(7 letters)

(8 letters)

WORDWORKS #11
"Whispering"

You are likely to discover at least 84 words hiding here. Find 50, you're the sly one; uncover 60, and you're quite the detective; 70 proves you to be a master sleuth!

(4 letters)   **(5 letters)**   **(6 letters)**

(7 letters)   **(9 letters)**

WORDWORKS #12
"Politician"

The word above is concealing at least 86 words. A score of 40 is good; 50, excellent; and 60 means you win by a landslide!

(4 letters)　　　　**(5 letters)**　　　　**(6 letters)**

(7 letters)

PLAYER'S CHOICE

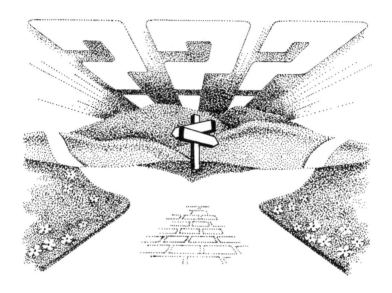

General Instructions

Whether it's politics, movies, sports, or art, you can test your acuity in the games that follow.

PLAYER'S CHOICE #1
Chain of Command

What's your political I.Q.? Pair up these U.S. Presidential candidates and their running mates and go to the top of the polls!

1. Richard Nixon	A.	Charles Curtis
2. Abraham Lincoln	B.	George Bush
3. Dwight Eisenhower	C.	Curtis LeMay
4. Harry S. Truman	D.	Estes Kefauver
5. Gerald Ford	E.	Martin Van Buren
6. Thomas Dewey	F.	Geraldine Ferraro
7. George McGovern	G.	Spiro Agnew
8. Franklin Delano Roosevelt	H.	John Nance Garner
9. George Wallace	I.	Lyndon B. Johnson
10. Warren G. Harding	J.	Dan Quayle
11. John F. Kennedy	K.	Patrick Lucey
12. Barry Goldwater	L.	Richard Nixon
13. Michael Dukakis	M.	Edmund Muskie
14. Theodore Roosevelt	N.	Theodore Roosevelt
15. Lyndon B. Johnson	O.	Hannibal Hamlin
16. Herbert Hoover	P.	Millard Fillmore
17. Jimmy Carter	Q.	Robert Dole
18. William McKinley	R.	Calvin Coolidge
19. Walter Mondale	S.	Hubert Humphrey
20. Ronald Reagan	T.	Earl Warren
21. John Anderson	U.	William Edward Miller
22. Hubert Humphrey	V.	Thomas Eagleton
23. Andrew Jackson	W.	Charles Fairbanks
24. George Bush	X.	Alben Barkley
25. Zachary Taylor	Y.	Lloyd Bentsen
26. Adlai Stevenson	Z.	Walter Mondale

PLAYER'S CHOICE #2
Famous Characters

If you're a film buff, this puzzle could be your ticket to success! Match the actors listed below with the name of the legendary movie characters they portrayed on the silver screen.

1. John Wayne
2. Humphrey Bogart
3. Kathleen Turner
4. Harrison Ford
5. Robert De Niro
6. Robert Redford
7. Anne Bancroft
8. Jimmy Stewart
9. James Caan
10. Dustin Hoffman
11. Henry Fonda
12. Barbra Streisand
13. Dudley Moore
14. Goldie Hawn
15. Bette Davis
16. Burt Lancaster
17. Vivien Leigh
18. Tom Hanks
19. Sean Connery
20. Jane Fonda
21. Diana Ross
22. Marlon Brando
23. Ingrid Bergman
24. Paul Newman
25. Liza Minnelli

A. Tom Joad
B. Margo Channing
C. Josh Baskin
D. Sonny Corleone
E. George Bailey
F. Barbarella
G. Stanley Kowalski
H. Scarlett O'Hara
I. James Bond
J. Mrs. Robinson
K. Jake LaMotta
L. Arthur
M. Butch Cassidy
N. Matty Walker
O. Ratso Rizzo
P. Hubbell Gardner
Q. Fanny Brice
R. Rooster Cogburn
S. Elmer Gantry
T. Sally Bowles
U. Rick Blaine
V. Anastasia
W. Billie Holliday
X. Private Benjamin
Y. Indiana Jones

PLAYER'S CHOICE #3
60s Television Shows

Is your favorite television rerun listed below? Match these 60s small screen hits with their star and shoot to the top of the Nielsens!

1.	Lassie	A.	Brian Kelly
2.	It's About Time	B.	Bob Denver
3.	Bachelor Father	C.	Martin Milner
4.	Flipper	D.	Carolyn Jones
5.	The Avengers	E.	Don Knotts
6.	My Mother the Car	F.	Patrick MacNee
7.	Gentle Ben	G.	John Forsythe
8.	Mission: Impossible	H.	Adam West
9.	The Addams Family	I.	Troy Donahue
10.	The Governor and J.J.	J.	Diahann Carroll
11.	Batman	K.	Guy Williams
12.	Wild Wild West	L.	Marty Ingels
13.	Adam 12	M.	Dan Dailey
14.	It Takes a Thief	N.	Buddy Ebsen
15.	The Green Hornet	O.	Patrick McGoohan
16.	Surfside Six	P.	Robert Conrad
17.	Lost in Space	Q.	Jerry Van Dyke
18.	Secret Agent	R.	Alan Young
19.	The Invaders	S.	Tommy Rettig
20.	I'm Dickens—He's Fenster	T.	Vince Edwards
21.	The Beverly Hillbillies	U.	Dennis Weaver
22.	The Andy Griffith Show	V.	Imogene Coca
23.	Gilligan's Island	W.	Robert Wagner
24.	Julia	X.	Peter Graves
25.	Mr. Ed	Y.	Roy Thinnes
26.	Ben Casey	Z.	Van Williams

PLAYER'S CHOICE #4
50s Sing Along

Match these 1950 chart-busters with the artists that made them memorable. A perfect score will have everyone singing your praises!

1.	Heartbreak Hotel	A.	Lloyd Price
2.	The Wayward Wind	B.	Frankie Avalon
3.	You Send Me	C.	Buddy Knox
4.	Smoke Gets in Your Eyes	D.	The Fleetwoods
5.	Stagger Lee	E.	Bobby Darin
6.	Poor Little Fool	F.	Tommy Edwards
7.	Wake Up Little Susie	G.	Perry Como
8.	Why	H.	Sam Cooke
9.	Tom Dooley	I.	Roger Williams
10.	Honeycomb	J.	Danny & the Juniors
11.	Tequila	K.	Pat Boone
12.	The Purple People Eater	L.	Ricky Nelson
13.	Young Love	M.	Elvis Presley
14.	Tammy	N.	Paul Anka
15.	It's All in the Game	O.	The Elegants
16.	Mr. Blue	P.	The Platters
17.	Witch Doctor	Q.	The Champs
18.	Party Doll	R.	Gogi Grant
19.	Round and Round	S.	The Crickets
20.	Mack the Knife	T.	Debbie Reynolds
21.	Little Star	U.	The Everly Brothers
22.	Diana	V.	Sheb Wooley
23.	At the Hop	W.	Tab Hunter
24.	Autumn Leaves	X.	The Kingston Trio
25.	April Love	Y.	Jimmie Rodgers
26.	That'll Be the Day	Z.	David Seville

PLAYERS CHOICE #5
The Classics

Movie mavens will be able to match up these award-winning films with their lead characters before the director says, "Roll 'em!"

1. My Fair Lady	A. Sam Spade
2. Mister Roberts	B. Norma Desmond
3. Top Hat	C. Rhett Butler
4. Sabrina	D. Jake Gittes
5. It's a Wonderful Life	E. Luke Skywalker
6. The Wizard of Oz	F. Elwood P. Dowd
7. Gone With the Wind	G. Blanche DuBois
8. Cat Ballou	H. Jim Stark
9. Casablanca	I. Linus Larrabee
10. All About Eve	J. Fanny Brice
11. The Maltese Falcon	K. Kid Shalleen
12. The African Queen	L. Margo Channing
13. Star Wars	M. Don Lockwood
14. The Hustler	N. Eliza Doolittle
15. Camelot	O. Scottie Ferguson
16. Singing In the Rain	P. Rick Blaine
17. The Godfather	Q. Ensign Pulver
18. Chinatown	R. George Bailey
19. Sunset Boulevard	S. Sally Bowles
20. Funny Girl	T. Eddie Felson
21. Rebel Without a Cause	U. Dorothy
22. Cabaret	V. Rose Sayer
23. A Streetcar Named Desire	W. King Arthur
24. Vertigo	X. Jerry Travers
25. Harvey	Y. Don Corleone

PLAYER'S CHOICE #6
A Rose by Any Other Name

Many famous people weren't born with the name they are known by. Below are some of those celebs; can you match them with their real names?

1.	Judy Garland	A.	Ann Leppert
2.	Mark Twain	B.	Leslie L. King, Jr.
3.	Rita Hayworth	C.	Rev. C. L. Dodgson
4.	Roy Rogers	D.	Samuel Clemens
5.	Alice Faye	E.	Martha Jane Burke
6.	Lauren Bacall	F.	Norma Jean Baker
7.	Gerald R. Ford	G.	Marion Morrison
8.	Marilyn Monroe	H.	Lucy Johnson
9.	Robert Goulet	I.	Florence N. Graham
10.	Calamity Jane	J.	Lucille Le Seuer
11.	Saki	K.	Leonard Slye
12.	Lewis Carroll	L.	Lily Chauchain
13.	Sarah Bernhardt	M.	Stanley Applebaum
14.	Joan Crawford	N.	Ehrich Weiss
15.	John Wayne	O.	Frances Gumm
16.	Ava Gardner	P.	Gladys Smith
17.	Harry Houdini	Q.	Betty Perske
18.	Elizabeth Arden	R.	Rosine Bernard
19.	Mary Pickford	S.	H. H. Munro
20.	Claudette Colbert	T.	Margarita Cansino

PLAYER'S CHOICE #7
The Sporting Life

Test your sports knowledge. You'll score by matching up these famous athletes with their chosen sport before the final buzzer sounds!

1. Gary Player	A. Billiards
2. Gordon Johncock	B. Indoor soccer
3. Janet Evans	C. Track & field
4. Willie Shoemaker	D. Diving
5. Gordie Howe	E. Horse racing
6. Debi Thomas	F. Gymnastics
7. Tatu	G. Swimming
8. Minnesota Fats	H. Football
9. Adrian Dantley	I. Golf
10. Alberto Tomba	J. Basketball
11. Florence Griffith Joyner	K. Chess
12. Warren Moon	L. Figure skating
13. Greg Louganis	M. Boxing
14. Mary Lou Retton	N. Auto racing
15. Roberto Duran	O. Poker
16. Mark Roth	P. Bowling
17. Greg Lemond	Q. Downhill racing
18. Bobby Fischer	R. Tennis
19. Amarillo Slim	S. Hockey
20. Chris Evert	T. Cycling

PLAYER'S CHOICE #8
Cold Feet

You'll have nothing to fear as you complete this puzzle; just match up the fears listed below with their clinical names. You can begin anytime and don't be scared—it's frightfully easy!

1. Fear of writing
2. Fear of vehicles
3. Fear of confinement
4. Fear of stealing
5. Fear of animals
6. Fear of thunder
7. Fear of strangers
8. Fear of marriage
9. Fear of colors
10. Fear of eating
11. Fear of solitude
12. Fear of spiders
13. Fear of people
14. Fear of small objects
15. Fear of water
16. Fear of dogs
17. Fear of sleep
18. Fear of money
19. Fear of heat
20. Fear of open spaces
21. Fear of mice
22. Fear of travel
23. Fear of work
24. Fear of time
25. Fear of talking

A. Phagophobia
B. Agoraphobia
C. Kleptophobia
D. Microphobia
E. Lalophobia
F. Hodophobia
G. Hydrophobia
H. Zoophobia
I. Amaxophobia
J. Thermophobia
K. Arachnophobia
L. Xenophobia
M. Cynophobia
N. Chromatophobia
O. Chronophobia
P. Musophobia
Q. Eremophobia
R. Claustrophobia
S. Hypnophobia
T. Ponophobia
U. Astraphobia
V. Anthropophobia
W. Graphophobia
X. Chrematophobia
Y. Gamophobia

PLAYER'S CHOICE #9
Classic Canvases

Your knowledge of famous painters will be tested with this puzzle! Match up the well-known artworks listed below with the artists who created these inspiring masterpieces.

1.	The Cradle	A.	Toulouse-Lautrec
2.	Mona Lisa	B.	Jackson Pollock
3.	Tahitian Women	C.	Claude Monet
4.	Dance At Bougival	D.	Henri Matisse
5.	American Gothic	E.	Vincent Van Gogh
6.	The Isles of Gold	F.	Edgar Degas
7.	Blackboard	G.	Norman Rockwell
8.	A Bar At the Folies-Bergere	H.	Mary Cassatt
9.	Lucifer	I.	Camille Pissarro
10.	The Talisman	J.	Paul Cezanne
11.	Dancers At the Bar	K.	Grant Wood
12.	The Young Hare	L.	Odilon Redon
13.	The Starry Night	M.	Jan Vermeer
14.	Weeping Woman	N.	Winslow Homer
15.	The Circus	O.	Berthe Morisot
16.	Reading "Le Figaro"	P.	Auguste Renoir
17.	Wild Poppies	Q.	Edouard Manet
18.	The Bather	R.	Albrecht Durer
19.	Easter Sunday	S.	Henri-Edmond Cross
20.	Moulin Rouge	T.	Leonardo Da Vinci
21.	The Parakeet and the Siren	U.	Pablo Picasso
22.	Closed Eyes	V.	Paul Serusier
23.	The Lacemaker	W.	Paul Gauguin
24.	Homecoming G.I.	X.	Andrew Wyeth
25.	The Card Players	Y.	Georges Seurat

PLAYER'S CHOICE #10
Hit or Myth

Pair up these deities in Roman mythology with the areas they were thought to have influenced and you'll make history!

1. Mercurius	A.	Goddess of the Moon
2. Bacchus	B.	God of Agriculture
3. Luna	C.	God of the Safely Gathered Harvest
4. Portunus	D.	Goddess of Marriage
5. Nona	E.	Goddess of Good Fortune
6. Orcus	F.	Guardian of Flocks and Herds
7. Salus	G.	Goddess of Growth
8. Tellus	H.	Goddess of Gardens
9. Libitina	I.	Goddess of Birth
10. Silvanus	J.	God of the Sun
11. Meditrina	K.	God of Trade and Industry
12. Consus	L.	Goddess of Springs and Wells
13. Amor	M.	Goddess of Freedom
14. Pax	N.	Protector of Health
15. Juno	O.	God of Fertility
16. Libertas	P.	God of Gateways
17. Sol	Q.	God of Fields and Woods
18. Pales	R.	God of the Underworld
19. Janus	S.	Goddess of the Healing Art
20. Flora	T.	Goddess of the Earth
21. Maia	U.	Goddess of Peace
22. Saturnus	V.	God of the House Entrance
23. Juturna	W.	Goddess of Interment
24. Fortuna	X.	God of Love
25. Spes	Y.	Goddess of Blossoming Flowers

LETTER PERFECT

General Instructions

In the puzzles that follow, the definitions give clues to words that begin and end with a designated letter. The last letter of the preceding word is also the first letter of the next word. Always work in the direction of the numbers. With these puzzles, it's okay to use proper nouns.

LETTER PERFECT #1

In this puzzle, the definitions give clues to words that begin and end with "T".

1. Series of sporting contests
2. Boston Harbor was a giant one
3. Written or typed copy
4. Young child
5. Television broadcast
6. Egyptian king
7. Violent commotion
8. Disorderly; unruly
9. Shining through
10. Matter on a printed page
11. Last will and _____
12. Equivalent
13. Musical instrument
14. Regulates temperature
15. Beginner Boy Scout
16. Drinking will quench this
17. To make lace
18. Johnny Carson showcase
19. Diplomacy
20. Lovers' rendezvous

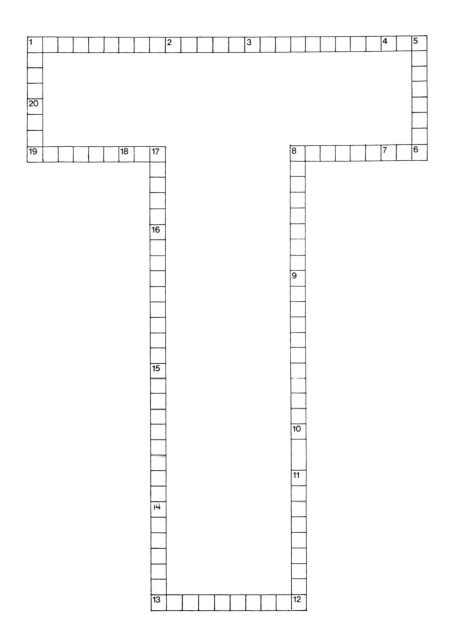

39

LETTER PERFECT #2

In this puzzle, the definitions give clues to words that begin and end with "T".

1. Easily understood; obvious
2. Substandard apartment building
3. _____ is fair play
4. Halloween custom
5. Fruit-filled pastry
6. Firm belief in person or thing
7. Unspoken; silent
8. One of three
9. Disposition; frame of mind
10. One who goes to the other side
11. In geometry, a nonintersecting line
12. Surgical procedure
13. Small corner tower
14. Temporary; passing with time
15. Writing paper fastened at one end
16. Absent without permission
17. William Hurt film, "The Accidental _____"
18. Multitalented individual, "triple _____"
19. Tense; not slack
20. Canvas shelter
21. Fish at the end of the rainbow

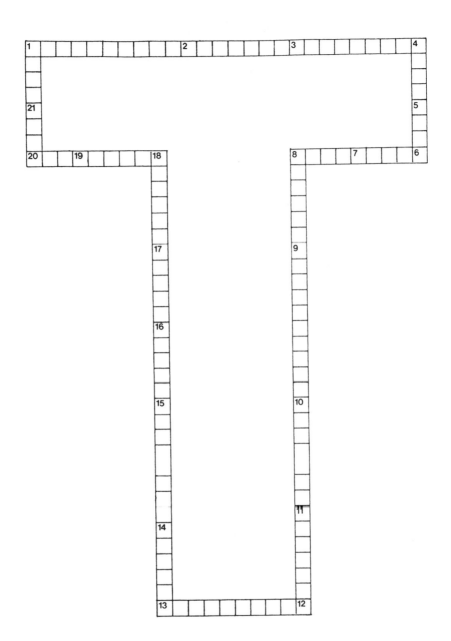

41

LETTER PERFECT #3

In this puzzle, the definitions give clues to words that begin and end with "E".

1. Baked clay containers; dishes
2. Large, imposing building
3. Small group of musicians
4. Keep apart; remove
5. Cut or etch letters on object
6. Shaky natural disaster
7. Vivid, forceful speech or writing style
8. Steal
9. Count one by one; list
10. Something that proves an allegation
11. Walkway along shoreline
12. Drive out evil spirits
13. Treat as equal
14. Roof edge
15. Slip by; pass
16. Get away from; flee
17. Free from blame
18. Tasteful and dignified manner
19. One with discriminating taste in food or wine
20. Give hope or confidence
21. French sandal or shoe
22. Bubbles in beverages
23. Teach; train
24. Insert opinions in factual article
25. Explain in greater detail

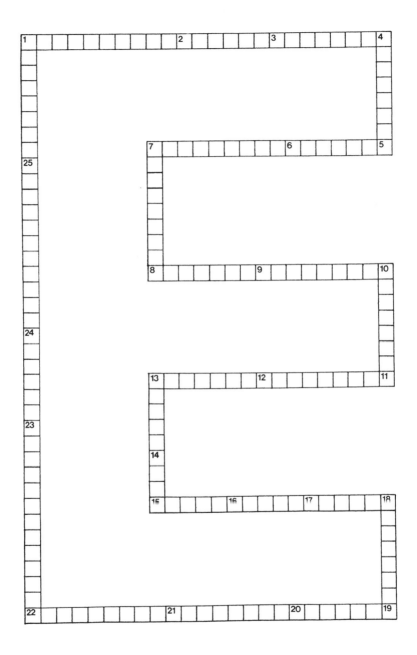

LETTER PERFECT #4

In this puzzle, the definitions give clues to words that begin and end with "E".

1. Embellish
2. Sight organ
3. The whole enchilada
4. Worker paid by another
5. Tolerate; bear
6. _____ out a living
7. Excited, enthusiastic manner
8. Hug; clasp in arms
9. Cast out; get rid of
10. Blow up
11. Weird; spooky
12. One's property and possessions
13. The front door is one
14. To exile or banish
15. Surrounded foreign territory
16. Costly
17. All qualified to vote
18. Compel; make happen
19. A letter is mailed in this
20. Mr. Ed, for example
21. Freedom from difficulty
22. Captain Kirk's starship
23. Popular men's magazine
24. Avoid or escape from
25. U.S. emblem
26. Outgoing waves
27. Prolonged banishment
28. Closing section of literary piece
29. Soft white fur
30. Qualified

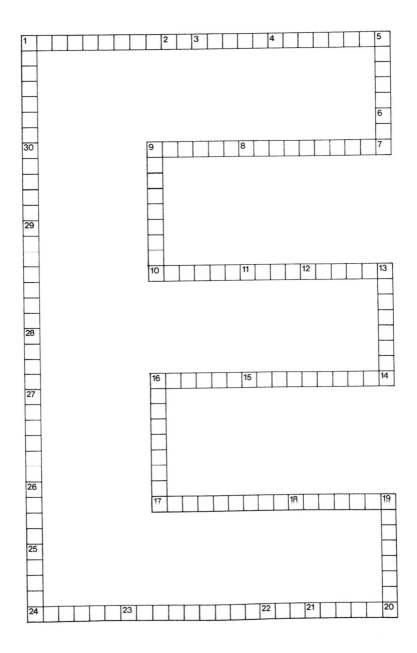

LETTER PERFECT #5

In this puzzle, the definitions give clues to words that begin and end with "L".

1. The Beatles' hometown
2. Garbage under layer of soil
3. Kind of evergreen shrub
4. Room deodorizer
5. Slander
6. In football, pass parallel to goal line
7. Part of the pea family
8. Political term for reciprocal voting
9. To classify as; identify
10. Opposite of conservative
11. Quiet; interval
12. Exact; precise
13. Miss Langtry's nickname
14. Faithful; true
15. Mel Gibson movie hit "_____ Weapon"
16. Lounge about
17. Listless; languid
18. Extension of jacket collar
19. Expressing feelings through song
20. Confined to a particular place
21. Uses correct reasoning

LETTER PERFECT #6

In this puzzle, the definitions give clues to words that begin and end with "N".

1. Female version of pajamas
2. Head (slang)
3. Has nine angles, nine sides
4. Women's stocking material
5. Male member of nobility
6. Wayne or fig
7. Colorless gas found in earth's atmosphere
8. Chemical element; component of all living things
9. Covers lap during meal
10. Famous blue-eyed thespian
11. Idea
12. Small ear of corn
13. Gary Cooper western "High _____"
14. One _____ indivisible
15. 18 + 1 =
16. 37th U.S. president
17. French general and emperor
18. Strikeout king Ryan
19. Day-old baby
20. Sister Kate is one
21. Country singer Willie _____
22. Uncharged atom part
23. Five-cent movie theater
24. Proton or neutron in atom's nucleus

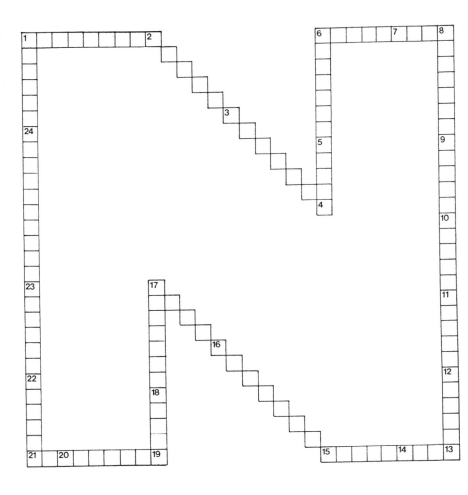

LETTER PERFECT #7

In this puzzle, the definitions give clues to words that begin and end with "H".

1. Hip and upper thigh
2. Seasoning; plant of mustard family with pungent root
3. Situated far above ground
4. Game involving moving from one compartment to another
5. Liquor; alcoholic beverage (slang)
6. Chopped mixture of cooked meat
7. Refuse fed to farm animals; swill
8. Canopied seat for riding on elephant or camel
9. Plant of lily family distinguished by bell-shaped flowers
10. Exclamation of praise to God
11. Stone or brick floor of fireplace
12. Very short distance
13. Turkish confection of seeds and nuts
14. Woody Allen character played by Mia Farrow
15. Make quiet or silent
16. Tahoe hotelier
17. Word with same spelling but different meaning and origin
18. From this moment on
19. Premonition; feeling about upcoming event
20. Cheer; shout of joy
21. "Leave It to Beaver" star _____ Beaumont
22. Part of racetrack between last turn and finish line
23. Physical and mental well-being
24. Fasten with hook or knot
25. Drug made of Indian hemp
26. Pen or coop for animals

50

LETTER PERFECT #8

In this puzzle, the definitions give clues to words that begin and end with "R".

1. Person skilled at telling stories or anecdotes
2. Appointed to hold funds of others
3. Unconfirmed story; hearsay
4. Male domestic fowl
5. Extreme harshness or severity
6. Cattle thief
7. Natural stream of water
8. Water-filled device for radiating heat
9. Santa Claus' transportation team
10. Bring to maturity by educating, nourishing
11. Loud, deep, rumbling sound
12. Warden who patrols government forests
13. Savior
14. Pistol with cylinder containing several cartridges
15. French painter
16. Tool of measurement
17. Continuing, bitter hate; ill will
18. Restaurant in style of German tavern
19. Wood or metal hinged vertically at ship's stern
20. Clinging rose
21. CBS news anchorman
22. Slender two-edged sword
23. Occur again after an interval
24. Reclaim or get back
25. Give or pay as due
26. Used to indicate direction and distance of object
27. Characterized by conformity, order

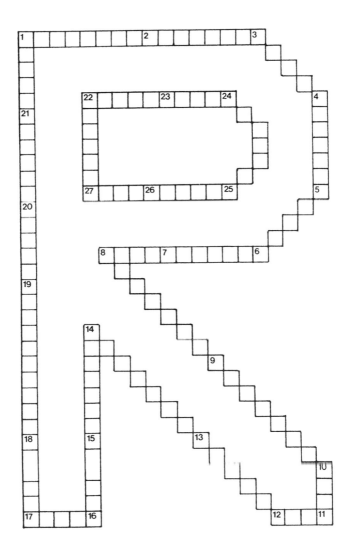

LETTER PERFECT #9

In this puzzle, the definitions give clues to words that begin and end with "D".

1. No longer living
2. Small dog with long body and short legs
3. Second king of Israel
4. Neglected; broken down
5. Hardest known mineral
6. Gadget; bauble
7. Wood nymph in Greek mythology
8. Stretch out; expand
9. Completely without
10. Intense fear, apprehension
11. Slight; treat without due respect
12. Sum of money divided among stockholders
13. Cartoon character _____ Bumstead
14. Automobile panel with instruments, gauges
15. The Magic Kingdom
16. Bomb that fails to explode
17. Without life
18. Misshapen
19. Country star Parton's theme park
20. Father
21. Move from higher to lower place
22. Document that states property transfer
23. Disagreement; clash
24. Mean, skulking coward
25. Member of Celtic religious order
26. Minor deity; partly divine

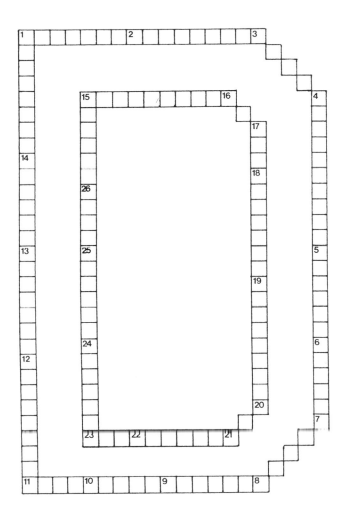

LETTER PERFECT #10

In this puzzle, the definitions give clues to words that begin and end with "S".

1. Disrespectful to things held sacred
2. Moved by natural feeling or impulse
3. Small telescope
4. Greek tragic dramatist
5. Phonograph needle
6. Quell; put down by force
7. Excessive; more than needed
8. Absence of
9. Working steadily; diligent
10. Strain; pressure
11. Advantageous coexistence of two dissimilar organisms
12. Italian violin craftsman
13. Contest involving common fund
14. Fond of study; attentive
15. Air carrier in skull opening to nasal cavities
16. Shameful; shocking
17. Brief, general review; summary
18. Characterized by false, malicious statements
19. Native of Switzerland
20. Having no backbone
21. Clandestine; secret

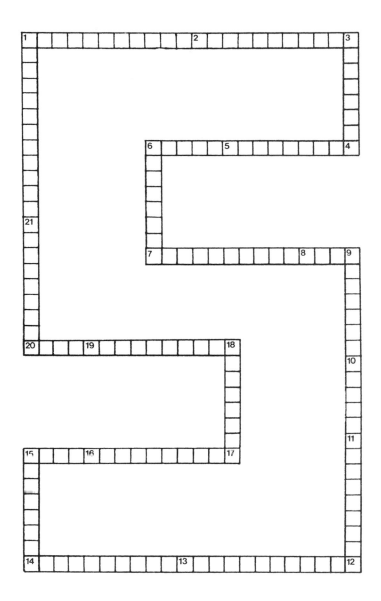

GREAT
BEGINNINGS

General Instructions

With these games, use the definitions to help you identify the words that begin with the specified letters.

GREAT BEGINNINGS #1
"IN"

Using the definitions listed below, identify these words that begin with IN.

1. Stimulus; motive — IN _____
2. True identity concealed or disguised — IN _____
3. Reliable; never wrong — IN _____
4. Establishment providing food and lodging — IN _____
5. Itemized list of goods — IN _____
6. Unafraid; bold; fearless — IN _____
7. Person who meddles in others' affairs — IN _____
8. Abnormal inability to sleep — IN _____
9. To receive as an heir — IN _____
10. Person confined to an institution or asylum — IN _____
11. Feebleness; weakness — IN _____
12. Measure of length; equal to $\frac{1}{12}$ foot — IN _____
13. To hurt or inflict physical harm — IN _____
14. Inactive; without power to move — IN _____
15. To examine by formal questioning — IN _____
16. Very young child; baby — IN _____
17. To sit on and hatch, as in eggs — IN _____
18. Raging fire; hellish — IN _____
19. Deep violet-blue — IN _____
20. The Hoosier state — IN _____
21. Group of foot soldiers — IN _____
22. Legally charge with a crime — IN _____
23. Colored liquid used for writing — IN _____

GREAT BEGINNINGS #2
"EX"

Using the definitions listed below, identify these words that begin with EX.

1. To dismiss; to _____ from school   EX _____
2. The way out   EX _____
3. Free from obligation; excused   EX _____
4. "Bill and Ted's _____ Adventure"   EX _____
5. Overstate; make something better than it is   EX _____
6. More or better than normal   EX _____
7. Test or quiz   EX _____
8. Process to discover something unknown   EX _____
9. Facial movement that reveals thoughts   EX _____
10. Minimize; apologize   EX _____
11. Second book of the Old Testament   EX _____
12. Costly; high priced   EX _____
13. Prolonged banishment   EX _____
14. Precise; accurate   EX _____
15. King Arthur's sword   EX _____
16. E.T. is one; alien being   EX _____
17. Enlarge; grow   EX _____
18. Great fatigue or weariness   EX _____
19. Highway for high-speed traffic   EX _____
20. One who carries out death penalty   EX _____
21. To send goods from one country to another   EX _____
22. Not an introvert   EX _____

GREAT BEGINNINGS #3
"QU"

Using the definitions listed below, identify these words that begin with QU.

1. Wet, boggy ground — QU_____
2. A group of four — QU_____
3. Bedcover stitched in patterns — QU_____
4. Sound a duck makes — QU_____
5. Shake; tremble — QU_____
6. Not noisy; hushed — QU_____
7. Angry dispute — QU_____
8. Wet, deep sand deposit — QU_____
9. Most powerful chess piece — QU_____
10. State of uncertainty; dilemma — QU_____
11. Society of Friends member — QU_____
12. Imposed isolation — QU_____
13. Small game bird — QU_____
14. Stone or slate is excavated from this — QU_____
15. Nazi collaborator; traitor — QU_____
16. Drink deeply and heartily — QU_____
17. Peculiarity — QU_____
18. Question; inquiry — QU_____
19. Line up — QU_____
20. Pleasingly odd and old-fashioned — QU_____
21. Subdue; allay — QU_____
22. Malaria treatment — QU_____
23. Yellowish apple-shaped fruit — QU_____
24. Football team leader — QU_____
25. Witty remark — QU_____

GREAT BEGINNINGS #4
"WA"

Using the definitions listed below, identify these words that begin with WA.

1. Erratic, eccentric, irrational (slang) WA _____
2. Thin, crisp cracker WA _____
3. Apple, celery, and walnut mixture WA _____
4. Carry or propel lightly WA _____
5. Female who serves restaurant patrons WA _____
6. Four-wheeled vehicle WA _____
7. Child without home or friends WA _____
8. Massive sea animal of the seal family WA _____
9. Small kangaroo WA _____
10. Roundish nut with two-lobed shell WA _____
11. Unchaste; lewd WA _____
12. Person looking on at a dance WA _____
13. Yellow substance secreted by bees WA _____
14. Fleshy flap of skin hanging from throat WA _____
15. Person's supply of clothes WA _____
16. Frame with ridged metal used for cleaning WA _____
17. Sing like a bird WA _____
18. Path taken by North American Indians on warlike expedition WA _____
19. First U.S. president WA _____
20. Sorcerer; wizard WA _____
21. Longing or urge to travel WA _____
22. Ballroom dance WA _____

GREAT BEGINNINGS #5
"SH"

Using the definitions listed below, identify these words that begin with SH.

1. Darkness cast upon a surface SH _____
2. Frozen watered fruit juice and sugar SH _____
3. English dramatist and poet; bard of Avon SH _____
4. Onionlike plant used for flavoring SH _____
5. Person who uses unethical or tricky methods SH _____
6. Fragment; broken piece SH _____
7. Cloth used to wrap corpse for burial SH _____
8. Neglect; evade an obligation SH _____
9. Shell fragments scattered by explosion SH _____
10. Fraud; imitation or counterfeit SH _____
11. Tomb of saint or revered person SII _____
12. British silver coin SH _____
13. Gesture indicating indifference SH _____
14. County's chief law enforcement officer SH _____
15. Plant; bush SH _____
16. Bunch of cut stalks of grain SH _____
17. Young pig SH _____
18. Used in baked goods SH _____
19. Sharp, piercing cry or scream SH _____
20. Small, long-tailed crustacean SH _____
21. Nagging, evil-tempered woman SH _____
22. Scrupulously avoid SH _____

GREAT BEGINNINGS #6
"PO"

Using the definitions listed below, identify these words that begin with PO.

1. Written expression, usually rhyming   PO _____

2. White, translucent, hard earthenware   PO _____

3. Spirit; ghost   PO _____

4. Device measuring pulse; lie detector   PO _____

5. To cook unbroken egg in water   PO _____

6. Hawaiian food made of mashed taro root   PO _____

7. Pope or high priest   PO _____

8. Flat portable case used for carrying   PO _____

9. Yellow powderlike cells on flower stamens   PO _____

10. Animal covered with sharp spines   PO _____

11. Painting of person, usually the face   PO _____

12. Position of body parts   PO _____

13. Popular card game   PO _____

14. Nonsense (slang)   PO _____

15. Hairdo; hair swept high off forehead   PO _____

16. Fast dance using specific music   PO _____

17. Body of men who assist sheriff   PO _____

18. The North Star   PO _____

19. Leading Communist Party committee   PO _____

20. Former mail delivery system using horses   PO _____

GREAT BEGINNINGS #7
"MA"

Using the definitions listed below, identify these words that begin with MA.

1. Authoritative order or command   MA _____
2. Small South American monkey   MA _____
3. Short love poem that can be set to music   MA _____
4. Hard metamorphic limestone   MA _____
5. Hypothetical inhabitant of Mars   MA _____
6. Man in charge of royal household   MA _____
7. One who chooses suffering rather than compromising principles   MA _____
8. Young Caroline Kennedy's pony   MA _____
9. Fat Tuesday; carnival day in New Orleans   MA _____
10. Manage or plan skillfully; scheme   MA _____
11. Intricate network of pathways   MA _____
12. Disease caused by infectious mosquito bite   MA _____
13. Tract of low, wet soft land   MA _____
14. Tragedy by Shakespeare   MA _____
15. Long distance or endurance contest   MA _____
16. Care of fingernails   MA _____
17. Rhythmic ballroom dance   MA _____
18. Cocktail made of gin and dry vermouth   MA _____
19. Purple and red mixture   MA _____

GREAT BEGINNINGS #8
"FO"

Using the definitions listed below, identify these words that begin with FO.

1. Young horse — FO _____
2. Lack of sense or rational conduct — FO _____
3. One's strong point — FO _____
4. Creamy sauce used for dipping — FO _____
5. Imitate for purposes of fraud — FO _____
6. Field team game played with pigskin — FO _____
7. Enemy; opponent — FO _____
8. Comment or reference at bottom of page — FO _____
9. For eternity; always; endlessly — FO _____
10. Bowl holding water in baptismal services — FO _____
11. Leaves, as of a plant or tree — FO _____
12. Tract of land covered by trees — FO _____
13. Small tongs or pincers for grasping, pulling — FO _____
14. Weakness in character; frailty — FO _____
15. Coarse food for cattle, horses — FO _____
16. Chain attached to watch — FO _____
17. To search for food or provisions — FO _____
18. Child found after parental abandonment — FO _____
19. Two weeks — FO _____
20. Hardened remains of ancient life — FO _____
21. Plant with small blue flowers — FO _____
22. Prohibit; rule against — FO _____

GREAT BEGINNINGS #9
"NO"

Using the definitions listed below, identify these words that begin with NO.

1. Flat, narrow strip of dough   NO _____
2. Longing for something long ago   NO _____
3. Eleventh month of calendar year   NO _____
4. Cut in edge or surface   NO _____
5. In the Bible, patriarch commanded to build an Ark   NO _____
6. Party's candidate in election   NO _____
7. Harmful to health   NO _____
8. Casually indifferent; without concern   NO _____
9. Clamor; din   NO _____
10. Special prayers and devotions   NO _____
11. Christmas expression of joy   NO _____
12. Swedish inventor of dynamite   NO _____
13. Loop formed in rope   NO _____
14. Small spout of hose   NO _____
15. Pen name; pseudonym   NO _____
16. Official authorized to attest documents   NO _____
17. Sugar and nut confection   NO _____
18. Brief written statement to aid memory   NO _____
19. Wanderer   NO _____
20. Functioning at night   NO _____
21. Person new to activity; apprentice   NO _____
22. Northern end of earth's axis   NO _____
23. Small knot or rounded lump   NO _____

GREAT BEGINNINGS #10
"TR"

Using the definitions listed below, identify these words that begin with TR.

1. Mark or line left by something that has passed   TR _____

2. Openwork structure of wooden strips   TR _____

3. Statue; prize awarded for achievement   TR _____

4. Group descended from common ancestor   TR _____

5. Unhappy, disastrous event   TR _____

6. Small window directly over door   TR _____

7. Caveman; hermit   TR _____

8. Net of strong canvas stretched on frame   TR _____

9. Calm, serene, free from stress   TR _____

10. Victory; success   TR _____

11. Bride's outfit of clothes, linen, jewelry, etc.   TR _____

12. Baglike net cast over fishing bank   TR _____

13. Short horizontal bar hung from ropes   TR _____

14. Fleshy edible fungi grown underground   TR _____

15. Surpass; excel; be superior to   TR _____

16. Group of three persons or things   TR _____

17. Emotional shock with lasting effects   TR _____

18. Something of little value   TR _____

19. Flat rectangular tool for smoothing plaster   TR _____

WORD CHASE

General Instructions

For the games that follow, circle the *capitalized* words hidden in the diagram. Words can run up or down, backwards, diagonally, or left to right. Time for each game: 20 minutes.

WORD CHASE #1
Country Flower Foray

ASTER
BETONY
BUTTERCUP
CHRYSANTHEMUM
CLEOME
DAFFODIL
DAHLIA
DAISY
DOGWOOD
FORSYTHIA

HYDRANGEA
INDIGO
IRIS
JOHNNY JUMP UP
JONQUIL
LARKSPUR
LILY
MAGNOLIA
OLEANDER
PANSY

PEONY
PETUNIA
PHLOX
POPPY
ROSE
SAGE
SEA HOLLY
SNAPDRAGON
VERBENA
ZINNIA

```
D A F F O D I L I U Q N O J
O I O E X R R E D N A E L O
G L R Y P U C R E T T U B H
W O S N A P D R A G O N E N
O N Y O N S E S U E T S T N
O G T E S K I T M Y O T O Y
D A H P Y R K O U R P O N J
A M I P I A E A Z N G P Y U
S E A H O L L Y N I I X O M
T I L L C A S A G E N A T P
E G I O G I D N I P B N R U
R L L X A I L H A D O R I P
Y A Y D O H Y D R A N G E A
C H R Y S A N T H E M U M V
```

WORD CHASE #2
Canine Conundrum

AFGHAN
AKITA
BASENJI
BEAGLE
BICHON FRISE
BORZOI
BOXER
BRITTANY
CAIRN Terrier
Japanese CHIN

DALMATIAN
GREYHOUND
LHASA APSO
MASTIFF
PEKINGESE
POMERANIAN
PUG
PULIK
SAINT Bernard
SALUKI

SCHNAUZER
SIBERIAN HUSKY
SILKY Terrier
SKYE Terrier
Fox TERRIER
WEIMARANER
Welsh CORGI
WHIPPET
VIZSLA

```
W  E  I  M  A  R  A  N  E  R  G  O  D  I
H  Y  N  A  I  T  A  M  L  A  D  E  A  N
I  K  A  T  O  X  F  F  I  T  S  A  M  U
P  S  F  N  S  A  L  U  K  I  Z  L  Y  L
P  U  G  I  A  P  N  L  R  K  H  V  N  A
E  H  H  A  Z  I  B  F  C  A  C  I  A  S
T  N  A  S  H  E  N  A  S  W  A  Z  T  C
E  A  N  C  A  O  F  A  S  P  I  S  T  H
R  I  O  G  H  C  A  I  R  E  R  L  I  N
R  R  L  C  O  P  L  E  M  E  N  A  R  A
I  E  I  R  S  K  I  L  U  P  M  J  B  U
E  B  G  O  Y  A  X  B  O  R  Z  O  I  Z
R  I  O  D  N  U  O  H  Y  E  R  G  P  E
E  S  E  G  N  I  K  E  P  B  O  X  E  R
```

WORD CHASE #3
Cat's Cradle

ABYSSINIAN
BALINESE
BIRMAN
BOMBAY
Japanese BOBTAIL
BURMESE
Maine COON
CORNISH REX

DEVON REX
EGYPTIAN MAU
HAVANA BROWN
KORAT
MANX
OCICAT
RAGDOLL
RUSSIAN BLUE

SCOTTISH FOLD
SHORTHAIR
SIAMESE
SOMALI
TONKINESE
TURKISH
  ANGORA

```
A  B  Y  S  S  I  N  I  A  N  S  O  M  E
R  H  U  C  I  L  A  M  O  S  H  I  N  S
O  A  A  R  A  G  D  O  L  L  O  T  C  E
G  V  M  O  M  A  N  X  A  I  R  O  D  N
N  A  N  C  E  E  D  A  B  A  T  N  E  I
A  N  A  I  S  L  S  I  M  T  H  K  V  L
H  A  I  C  E  C  R  E  I  B  A  I  O  A
S  B  T  A  T  M  O  S  Z  O  I  N  N  B
I  R  P  T  A  P  H  O  M  B  R  E  R  O
K  O  Y  N  R  F  E  A  N  A  I  S  E  C
R  W  G  C  O  R  N  I  S  H  R  E  X  A
U  N  E  L  K  D  O  P  Y  A  B  M  O  B
T  A  D  E  U  L  B  N  A  I  S  S  U  R
```

WORD CHASE #4
Everything's Coming Up Roses

CHINA DOLL
CINDERELLA
CONFIDENCE
DON JUAN
DUET
FOXY LADY
FRAGRANT CLOUDS
GARNETTE

HAPPY
INTRIGUE
LOVE
LUVVIE
MEDALLION
MON CHERI
NEW DAWN
OLE

PINK FAVORITE
PROMINENT
RED DEVIL
SCARLET KNIGHT
SNOW BRIDE
SUN FLARE
YANKEE DOODLE

```
S  D  U  O  L  C  T  N  A  R  G  A  R  F
L  N  O  I  L  L  A  D  E  M  D  U  E  T
O  F  O  X  Y  L  A  D  Y  P  I  C  L  H
V  S  C  W  A  Y  D  U  G  I  T  I  D  G
E  U  M  A  B  E  I  A  C  N  E  N  O  I
L  N  Q  O  V  R  R  D  E  K  A  D  O  N
L  F  U  I  N  N  I  N  X  F  N  E  D  K
O  L  L  A  E  C  I  D  D  A  W  R  E  T
D  A  X  T  Y  M  H  O  E  V  A  E  E  E
A  R  T  P  O  A  N  E  N  O  D  L  K  L
N  E  P  R  I  J  A  D  R  R  W  L  N  R
I  A  P  L  U  V  V  I  E  I  E  A  A  A
H  C  E  A  E  U  G  I  R  T  N  I  Y  C
C  O  N  F  I  D  E  N  C  E  O  L  E  S
```

WORD CHASE #5
Movie Comedians

ABBOTT, Bud
ALDA, Alan
ALLEN, Woody
BALL, Lucille
BROOKS, Albert
BROOKS, Mel
CHAPLIN, Charlie
COSTELLO, Lou
CRYSTAL, Billy
DAY, Doris
DREYFUSS, Richard
FALK, Peter
FIELDS, W. C.

GARR, Teri
GRANT, Cary
HANKS, Tom
HAWN, Goldie
HOPE, Bob
KAHN, Madeleine
KEATON, Buster
KEATON, Michael
LEE, Spike
LEMMON, Jack
LLOYD, Harold
LOY, Myrna
MARTIN, Steve
MARX Brothers

MATTHAU, Walter
MAY, Elaine
MIDLER, Bette
MOORE, Dudley
MULL, Martin
MURPHY, Eddie
POWELL, William
SELLERS, Peter
SKELTON, Red
TOMLIN, Lily
WEST, Mae
WILDER, Gene
WILLIAMS, Robin

N	I	T	R	A	M	E	C	H	A	P	L	I	N
O	E	G	A	R	R	E	L	D	I	M	A	P	O
T	P	B	R	O	O	K	S	W	E	S	T	O	M
L	O	Y	O	L	S	R	E	L	L	E	S	W	M
E	H	M	X	R	A	M	U	R	P	H	Y	E	E
K	W	K	L	M	A	T	T	H	A	U	R	L	L
S	I	L	K	I	T	X	A	W	F	M	C	L	D
D	L	A	E	O	N	E	N	Y	O	A	O	E	R
L	L	F	B	L	E	O	A	S	N	Y	S	N	E
E	I	B	L	A	L	D	T	H	D	N	T	O	Y
I	A	U	B	E	L	I	N	A	A	H	E	T	F
F	M	O	E	A	A	L	A	N	E	A	L	A	U
A	S	K	O	O	R	B	R	K	E	K	L	E	S
W	I	L	D	E	R	I	G	S	T	X	O	K	S

WORD CHASE #6
Baseball Greats

AARON, Hank
ALEXANDER, Grover Cleveland
BRETT, George
CAMPANELLA, Roy
CAREW, Rod
COBB, Ty
DEAN, Dizzy
DIMAGGIO, Joe
FOXX, Jimmie

GROVE, Lefty
HAFEY, Chick
JACKSON, Shoeless Joe
KOUFAX, Sandy
LOMBARDI, Ernie
MACK, Connie
MCCOVEY, Willie
MIZE, Johnny
OTT, Mel
PALMER, Jim
REISER, Pete

RICE, Jim
ROBINSON, Jackie
ROUSH, Edd
RUTH, Babe
RYAN, Nolan
SCHMIDT, Mike
SPEAKER, Tris
TERRY, Bill
VANCE, Dazzy
VAUGHAN, Arky
YASTRZEMSKI, Carl

```
A Y E F A H L O M B A R D I
A L N O S K C A J E N A Y R
R A E X U N I L S O G Z O N
O L O X C Y R E S I E R Z E
N L I O A E C N A H G U A V
O E G S M N I M C C O V E Y
S N G L A B D R E K A E P S
N A A V O E X E T Y W F C A
I P M R A A Z T R E H H O Y
B M I N F I E R R S M A B R
O A D U M R I A U I H T U R
R C O B B C C O D G R O V E
I K S M E Z R T S A Y O T T
```

WORD CHASE #7
Oscar Winners: Best Supporting Actress

ASTOR, Mary
BAINTER, Fay
BAXTER, Anne
BERGMAN, Ingrid
DARWELL, Jane
DENNIS, Sandy
DUKE, Patty
GORDON, Ruth
GRAHAME, Gloria
GRANT, Lee
HAWN, Goldie
HAYES, Helen

HOLM, Celeste
HULL, Josephine
HUNT, Linda
HUNTER, Kim
HUSTON, Anjelica
JONES, Shirley
KEDROVA, Lila
LANGE, Jessica
LEACHMAN, Cloris
MCCAMBRIDGE, Mercedes
MCDANIEL, Hattie

MORENO, Rita
REED, Donna
REVERE, Anne
RUTHERFORD, Margaret
SMITH, Maggie
STAPLETON, Maureen
STEENBURGEN, Mary
STREEP, Meryl
TREVOR, Claire

```
L  A  N  G  E  K  U  D  E  N  N  I  S  N
E  M  A  H  A  R  G  R  E  T  N  U  H  E
A  L  E  I  N  A  D  C  M  H  O  L  M  G
C  L  E  M  O  S  C  A  R  A  S  T  O  R
H  E  R  O  D  I  M  E  R  W  O  N  K  U
M  W  E  R  R  S  X  O  N  O  T  E  B
A  R  V  E  O  X  O  T  V  T  N  H  D  N
N  A  E  N  G  E  R  F  E  A  U  T  R  E
A  D  R  O  A  R  S  L  R  N  M  I  O  E
M  S  T  R  E  E  P  G  T  E  O  M  V  T
G  E  O  T  N  A  R  G  X  M  H  S  A  S
R  Y  X  O  T  F  A  B  A  I  N  T  E  R
E  A  J  S  H  U  S  T  O  N  L  L  U  H
B  H  M  C  C  A  M  B  R  I  D  G  E  R
```

WORD CHASE #8
Oscar Winners: Best Supporting Actor

ALBERTSON, Jack
AMECHE, Don
BALSAM, Martin
BEGLEY, Ed
BRENNAN, Walter
BURNS, George
BUTTONS, Red
COBURN, Charles
CRISP, Donald
DE NIRO, Robert
DOUGLAS, Melvyn

DUNN, James
FITZGERALD,
 Barry
GIELGUD, John
GREY, Joel
GWENN, Edmund
HEFLIN, Van
HOUSEMAN, John
HUSTON, Walter
HUTTON, Timothy
IVES, Burl

MATTHAU, Walter
MILLS, John
NICHOLSON, Jack
ROBARDS, Jason
SCHILDKRAUT,
 Joseph
USTINOV, Peter
WALKEN,
 Christopher
YOUNG, Gig

WORD CHASE #9
The Only Way To Fly

AEROPERU
Air ALASKA
Air CANADA
AMERICAN
British CALEDONIA
CATHAY
CHINA Air
CONTINENTAL
DELTA
EASTERN
EL AL

FINN AIR
GULF Air
KLM
LOT
LAN CHILE
LUFTHANSA
MEXICANA
MIDWAY Airlines
OLYMPIC
PSA
PIEDMONT

QANTAS
SINGAPORE Air
SKY West
SOUTHWEST
SWISS Air
TACA
THAI
TWA
US AIR
UNITED

A E R O P E R U Y A H T A C

S I N G A P O R E T U Q O U

N E I R A C A T N S A N L Q

A L L X E G H O A I T F Y A

H A C I U Y M I N I T I M N

T L O L H D R O N M S N P T

F C F S E C D E N A E N I A

U U A I V E N A A S W A C S

L N P N L T C A K S H I L W

A I E A A I D Y L T T R A I

T T C L R D T A M B U E I S

L E W E V O A S P R O C R S

E D M A L E G A L A S K A N

D A N A C I X E M I D W A Y

WORD CHASE #10
It's All Greek to Me

ADONIS
AEOLUS
ANDROMEDA
APHRODITE
ARGUS
ATLAS
ATHENA
CASSIOPEIA
CASTOR
CLYTEMNESTRA
DEMETER

DIONYSUS
ERIS
EROS
EUTERPE
GAEA
GANYMEDE
HEBE
HERA
HERCULES
HERMES
HYDRA

LACHESIS
LEDA
NIKE
NIOBE
PLUTO
RHEA
TANTALUS
THALIA
THETIS
ZEUS

```
C A A I E P O I S S A C O D
L A D B S U L A T N A T E I
Y T E O T I T U L P L U T O
T H L A N H A E O L U S I N
E E V I G I A Y R U E M D Y
M N O A R O S L S P A C O S
N A L A C H E S I S E A R U
E R E T E M E D R A R S H S
S E A S A L T A E V E T P I
T R O R U T S E A M I O A T
R L H C D G U C R A Y R T E
A I R E N Y R E B O I N K H
Z E U S A T H A E N S I A T
H E R A D E M O R D N A N G
```

STIR CRAZIES

General Instructions

For the games that follow, find the words that go in the boxes on the right. Select a word from the first column, combine its letters with those from a word in the second column, and rearrange the letters to spell the word that goes in the box on the right. In each game, one's been done to help you get started.

STIR CRAZIES #1
Mixed Fruit

In the boxes on the right, find the names of eight fruits. The first and last letters of each fruit are underlined.

C̶A̶P̶	RE	PEACH
GAP	HER	
TOO	NOR	
PLANE	MAT	
WOMEN	LOUT	
CANAPE	LATER	
AGE	PIPE	
CRY	H̶E̶	

STIR CRAZIES #2
Clothes Make the Man

In the boxes on the right, find eight pieces of clothing and/or accessories comprising a single ensemble for a man, each consisting of two words.

HONORS	S̶L̶A̶N̶T̶	TAN SLACKS
PINT	ZEAL	
S̶A̶C̶K̶	WEBS	
SOAKS	VOTES	
RUBBLE	SHIRK	
THERE	PIETY	
MANOR	CLERGY	
AISLE	BALLET	

STIR CRAZIES #3
Scary Possibilities

Horror novel fans can find eight books by Stephen King in the boxes on the right. The first letters of each word in the title are underlined.

~~THAT~~	SHIN	THE STAND
HEATED	RISER	
TRICE	MATEY	
FATTER	HIGH	
THREAT	MELT	
REPAST	~~SEND~~	
LASSO	WORKED	
TENNIS	DOZEN	

STIR CRAZIES #4
Lights, Camera, Action!

Roll 'em, movie buffs, and find eight big flicks of the '80s in the boxes on the right. The first letters of each two-word title are underlined.

~~ABODE~~	DEUCES	BODY HEAT
SMEAR	VETCH	
CHAT	LETTER	
RAN	TWEEDS	
TACITLY	~~THY~~	
SLAW	HID	
TIRED	ANTIC	
READ	MINA	

STIR CRAZIES #5
Elementary, Dear Solver

Hey, super sleuths, find eight famous fictional detectives in the mystery boxes on the right. The first letters of the person's first and last name are underlined.

WREN	ARMS	NANCY DREW
HAIR	EARN	
EON	CANDY	
SIMPLE	CHALKS	
DAMP	CHANCEL	
CROUPIER	SEAS	
NICER	FLOWER	
SCHOLAR	HELOT	

STIR CRAZIES #6
Up a Tree

Your climb to the top will be successful if you find the eight trees hidden in the boxes on the right. The first and last letters of each tree are underlined.

RAP	NAB	
YORE	MANGO	
ODOR	OMENS	
ANY	LOP	POPLAR
HAY	MAIN	
YEARN	SCAM	
GOAL	BIRCH	
PRIM	DEW	

STIR CRAZIES #7
Strictly for the Birds

Good eggs will find eight familiar birds nesting in the boxes on the right. The first and last letters of each word have been underlined.

WALL	CLAD	
RASP	PRIDE	
SNAP	POKER	
NOG	SOW	SWALLOW
RAIN	GRAPE	
SUPER	PIE	
COWED	ROW	
DIRT	SACK	

STIR CRAZIES #8
Rhythmic Riddles

In the boxes below are the scrambled names of eight musical instruments. Note: The first and last letters of each word are underlined.

LOAN	PEONS	
PEELING	AROMA	
RICE	MIND	MANDOLIN
RAGE	CANNOT	
BROOM	ACID	
CHIN	LOCKS	
HOAX	TONE	
CROON	LINT	

STIR CRAZIES #9
Just Desserts

Eight exotic desserts await those with an appetite for greater challenges. Combine the letters from a word in column one with those from a word in columns two and three. Each is a two-word name, and only the *first* letter of both names is underlined.

			PEACH BOMBE
PURGE	CAB	COP	
BABE	REACT	TIARA	
THUS	HEM	NOEL	
SOLE	ORGAN	MOIST	
CASE	MUFF	ROLES	
ORT	POUR	BAND	
MAP	FLAP	HEEL	
CREAM	DID	BEES	

STIR CRAZIES #10
The Write Stuff

Eight great American authors, past and present, are waiting to be discovered in the boxes on the right. Combine the letters from a word in column one with those from a word in columns two and three. The first letter of the author's first and last name is underlined.

			WILLIAM STYRON
WANTY	OAT	CAKE	
HARM	TERN	WALL	
RULE	MIST	EACH	
AIR	MILIEU	ATTACH	
FRANK	JEST	ROIL	
PENS	WHIMSY	DEWY	
GREEN	GERM	NEAT	
MILLER	WELL	RUBE	

STORY BUILDERS

General Instructions

For these games, add a letter to the underlined letter or letters to complete the blank word that follows. Then, using the same letters, add still another letter to complete the next word, and so on. Letters may or may not appear in the same sequence each time, but each word will always contain the letters from the previous word in addition to the new letter you add.

STORY BUILDER #1
The Rest Is Up to You

" <u>I</u> <u>T</u> really is a shame to __ __ __ around and feel that life is over because you had to retire," Mona admonished Jack. "In fact, it's the __ __ __ __ ! Why not find a hobby, read a book, or plan some __ __ __ __ __ ? Or maybe you should see our __ __ __ __ __ __ . I'm sure Father O'Malley can offer you some __ __ __ __ __ __ __ from your sorrow over getting too much rest."

STORY BUILDER #2
Winner Takes All

"To <u>B</u> <u>E</u> honest, Sam, you've disappointed me," Joey said. "You lost the __ __ __ , but your __ __ __ __ is still outstanding. Now you expect me to stand here with __ __ __ __ __ breath while you __ __ __ __ __ __ the ethics of gambling. Well, you can just forget it, pal, I refuse to be __ __ __ __ __ __ __ for putting the squelch on a welch!"

STORY BUILDER #3
Charles Darwin, Phone Home!

" <u>P</u> <u>A</u>, you've known me a long time," grumbled Ma, "and by now it should be obvious that I'm not __ __ __ to pay __ __ __ __ attention to all your foolish notions. You __ __ __ __ __ constantly about science and evolution, neither of which you know very well, and I find it very upsetting when you __ __ __ __ __ __ with theories like the one you mentioned yesterday: that man is the least intelligent __ __ __ __ __ __ __ of all!"

STORY BUILDER #4
A Legend in His Own Mind

"I simply <u>D</u> <u>O</u> not understand why you think you're better than everyone else," Ben mused, slowly shaking his head in wonder as he studied Eugene. "Let's face it, you eat, sleep, drink, and walk on the same _ _ _ that a common cur _ _ _ _ , yet you've always _ _ _ _ _ as someone superior. In my opinion, you'd make a perfect _ _ _ _ _ _ , Eugene, and I _ _ _ _ _ _ _ this character flaw the first time we met. The crown you were wearing was a dead giveaway!"

STORY BUILDER #5
Career Oriented

"<u>N</u> <u>O</u> individual, not even a very bright _ _ _ , can give you a foolproof formula for success, Marsha," Mike said patiently, "but even a _ _ _ _ like yours truly can offer some pointers. That company party we attended last night, for instance, makes me _ _ _ _ _ to think you won't get the promotion you're after. It just doesn't look good when you fall asleep on the shoulder of the _ _ _ _ _ _ you're sitting beside at dinner, especially when it's your boss. And I'm sure someone in his position _ _ _ _ _ _ _ the merit of promoting an employee who _ _ _ _ _ _ _ _ , 'I prefer that you call me Marsha,' when he asks if he can call you a cab!"

STORY BUILDER #6
What You See Is What You Get

<u>A</u> <u>T</u> what point does a mediocre painting suddenly become a great work of _ _ _ ? Usually it happens when self-appointed critics start to _ _ _ _ and rave about a work's

redeeming value, focusing on features that are invisible to most of us. In this way, they _ _ _ _ _ us to doubt our own judgment, and _ _ _ _ _ _ their power to influence our tastes and buying habits.

Obviously it takes a _ _ _ _ _ _ _ amount of self-confidence and strength to say, "My _ _ _ _ _ _ _ _ is as valid as yours, Mr. Critic, and many of those _ _ _ _ _ _ _ _ _ you're calling art aren't on a par with preschool finger painting!"

STORY BUILDER #7
Who Are We To Judge?

"Hi, <u>P</u> <u>A</u>," the young man greeted his father. "I just ran into your old _ _ _ , Judge Mann, and he was so _ _ _ _ _ I hardly recognized him! I guess he saw me do a double-take, because he smiled and said, 'I'm not sick, my boy, just tired. I've been hearing so many _ _ _ _ _ lately, I sometimes find myself _ _ _ _ _ _ when key witnesses are testifying! I won't be surprised if a higher court _ _ _ _ _ _ _ a lot of my recent rulings.' Then he smiled wearily and added, 'Perhaps we judges should have settled for being _ _ _ _ _ _ _ _ . Then we could just listen to the accused's confession, and leave the judgment to someone much more qualified!' "

STORY BUILDER #8
A Hard One To Fathom

<u>A</u> walk along this lonely beach is _ _ mystifying as the _ _ _ that watches us in cryptic green silence. Here, where countless _ _ _ _ have witnessed the _ _ _ _ _ and laughter of earlier generations, few _ _ _ _ _ _ remain of times that were. It is this great sense of aloneness,

I think, that _ _ _ _ _ _ _ the mystique pertaining
to oceans, and maintains a certain mysterious appeal
_ _ _ _ _ _ _ _ as the sea, herself.

STORY BUILDER #9
In Deep Water

"Like it O R not, Harold," Hazel said, "I've manned these
oars long enough. It's time for you to _ _ _ ."

Noticing how far they were to shore, he cagily replied,
"Okay, but mark my _ _ _ _ , tomorrow you'll regret not
getting more exercise."

"More? I'm already so tired that I'd _ _ _ _ _ if I sud-
denly had to swim," Hazel snapped. "But your concern
makes me _ _ _ _ _ _ _ , Harold, wouldn't you be healthier
if you occasionally exercised more than just your
prerogative?"

"There you go," Harold hissed. "You always manage to
turn our outings into total _ _ _ _ _ _ _ , and now
you're doing it again!"

Matters only _ _ _ _ _ _ _ _ from that point, and
their canoe trip became just another paddle between the
sexes.

STORY BUILDER #10
Food for Thought

Some believe that knowledge, P E R se, has no value unless
it is shared. Only then, they maintain, can humankind
_ _ _ _ its benefits. Every good seed of thought that is
sown and cultivated in the beds of fertile minds then be-
comes a _ _ _ _ _ of wisdom. Thinkers, in turn, can
_ _ _ _ _ _ its benefits with others, expand upon it, and
perhaps someday _ _ _ _ _ _ _ it in new, exciting ways.
Such is the story of growth.

90

SAY IT AGAIN, SAM

General Instructions

In each of the following grids, five synonyms or words similar in meaning can be found. Following the example and using the clue letters provided in each puzzle, complete the words.

Example:

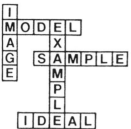

IMAGE / MODEL / EXAMPLE / SAMPLE / IDEAL crossword

#1

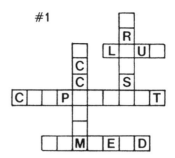

#2

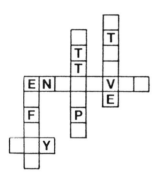

#3

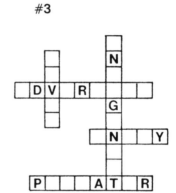

#4

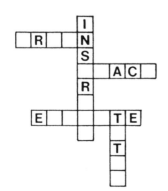

#5

92

#6

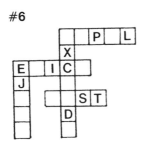

#7

#8

#9

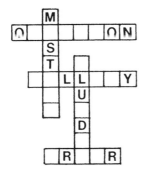

#10

93

TAKE FIVE

General Instructions

In the grids that follow, fill in each box with an answer beginning with the letter above each of the five columns, and fitting the category at the left of each row. Try to list one answer in every box, although some boxes may have more than one correct answer.

TAKE FIVE #1

	S	C	O	R	E
AMERICAN INDIANS					
ICE CREAM FLAVORS					
BIBLICAL FIGURES					
VEGETABLES					
COLORS					

TAKE FIVE #2

	R	G	P	S	B
CHEESES					
FEMALE SINGERS					
BODIES OF WATER					
MEN'S FIRST NAMES					
CARD GAMES					

TAKE FIVE #3

	D	A	B	S	P
STATE CAPITALS					
CARTOON CHARACTERS					
TELEVISION SOAP OPERAS					
PROFESSIONS					
CARY GRANT MOVIES					

TAKE FIVE #4

	C	H	A	M	P
MOVIE TITLES					
NUTS					
TREES					
7-LETTER NOUNS					
PRO FOOTBALL PLAYERS					

TAKE FIVE #5

	W	S	C	B	R
PROFESSIONAL GOLFERS					
SEAFOOD					
TELEVISION NEWSCASTERS					
BROADWAY MUSICALS					
WORLD CAPITALS					

TAKE FIVE #6

	T	S	M	R	C
TELEVISION SLEUTHS					
FAIRY TALES					
CHILD STARS					
DANCES					
MODES OF TRAVEL					

TAKE FIVE #7

	G	R	E	A	T
MOVIE STARS					
FLOWERS					
CAR/TRUCK MODELS					
FOREIGN COUNTRIES					
RIVERS					

TAKE FIVE #8

	C	M	O	G	S
SPORTSCASTERS					
MIXED DRINKS					
BIRDS					
MINERALS					
CANDY BRANDS					

TAKE FIVE #9

	M	A	D	E	N
PAST OR PRESENT WORLD LEADERS					
INVENTORS					
MAMMALS					
ELVIS PRESLEY SONGS					
OPERAS					

TAKE FIVE #10

S					
A					
C					
E					
G					
	HERBS	US ASTRONAUTS	MAGAZINES	FRUITS	POETS

ANSWERS

TRICKY TRIOS

#1, "EGR"

A score of 15 is fine; 18, first-rate; 22, fantastic!

begrime, begrudge, biodegradable, degrade, degranulation, degree, degression, disintegrate, egregious, egress, egret, integrand, integrate, integrity, integrodifferential, legroom, megrim, negritude, peregrine, regress, regret, regroup, segregate, telegram, telegraph

#2, "OXY"

Find 12, you're batting 1.000; 15, you're an all-star; 17, you're a hall of famer!

boxy, deoxycorticosterone, deoxygenate, deoxyribose, doxy, doxycycline, epoxy, foxy, hydroxyl, oxyacetylene, oxyacid, oxycephaly, oxygen, oxyhemoglobin, oxymoron, oxysulfide, oxytetracycline, oxytocic, oxytone, oxyuriasis, proxy

#3, "ADI"

Finding 60 words is dandy; 70, fantastic; 80, phenomenal!

adiabetic, adieu, adios, adipose, adit, amantadine, anadiplosis, arcading, armadillo, badinage, barricading, beading, beheading, besteading, brigadier, brocading, butadiene, cadi, caladium, cannonading, cascading, circadian, contradict, contradistinguish, degrading, eradicate, escalading, evading, extradite, fading, freeloading, gladiator, gladiola, gliadin, goading, gradin, grading, granadilla, haggadist, heading, hexadic, invading, irradiate, irradicable, jading, kneading, lading, leading, loading, masquerading, monadic, muscadine, nadir, nomadism, paladin, palladium, paradigm, parading, paradise, peccadillo, persuading, pleading, radial, radiant, radiator, radical, radio, radiology, radish, radium, radix, readily, reading, sadiron, sadist, shading, sporadic, spreading, stadium, steadily, threading, toadies, tornadic, trading, tradition, traditor, treading, triadic, wadi, wading

#4, "ERT"

Finding 75 words is good; 90, excellent; 100, extraordinary!

advertise, alert, aperture, appertain, ascertain, assert, avert, berth, bertha, certes, certain, certificate, certify, certiorari, chert, concert, concertina, concertino, concertmaster, concerto, controvert, convert, convertible, convertiplane, covert, culvert, desert, desertion, dessert, disconcert, divert, diverticulitis, diverticulosis, diverticulum, divertimento, divertissement, entertain, evert, exert, expert, extrovert, fertile, fertilizer, filbert, gilbert, hypertension, hyperthermia, hyperthyroid, hypertonic, hypertrophy, inadvertent, inert, insert, intertexture, intertribal, intertropical, intertwine, introvert, invertase, libertarian, libertine, liberty, nerts, obvert, offertory, overt, overtake, overtax, overthrow, overtime, overtone, overtop, overtrain, overtrick, overtrump, overture, overturn, pert, pertain, pertinacious, pertinent, perturb, pertussis, pervert, poverty, property, puberty, revert, sertularian, stertor, subvert, summertime, supertanker, supertax, supertonic, tertial, tertian, tertiary, travertine, undertaker, underthings, undertone, undertrained, vert, vertebra, vertebrate, vertex, vertical, verticillate, vertiginous, vertigo, vertu, watertight, wert, wintertime

#5, "AZI"

A score of 10 is terrific; 12, great; 15, tops!

amazing, azide, azimuth, azine, blazing, brazier, brazilwood, crazier, dazing, fazing, feazing, gazing, glazier, grazing, hazier, lazier, magazine, razing, triazine

#6, "OQU"

A score of 8 is par; 10, a birdie; 14, an eagle!

baroque, coquette, coquille, coquina, coquito, croquet, croquette, croquinole, eloquent, hydroquinone, loquacious, loquat, moquette, roque, roquelaure, toque

#7, "ICO"

A score of 65 words is outstanding; 75, magnificent; 82 or better, pure genius!

alnico, anticoagulant, anticonvulsant, apricot, beccafico, bellicose, bicolor, biconcave, biconvex, bicorn, bicorporal, bicostate, calico, chalicosis, chalicothere, chico, chicory, corticoid, corticolous, corticospinal, dicotyledon, epicotyl, helicoid, helicon, helicopter, icon, iconoclast, iconography, iconoscope, iconostasis, lamellicorn, lexicology, lexicon, licorice, limicoline, longicorn, lumbricoid, machicolate, magnifico, manicotti, manticore, maricolous, medico, medicolegal, minicomputer, multicolored, nicotiana, nicotine, orthicon, particolored, physicochemical, picogram, picoline, picornavirus, picosecond, picot, picotee, politico, portico, ricochet, ricotta, rupicolous, saxicolous, semicolon, semicomatose, semiconductor, semiconscious, silicon, silicone, silicosis, stereopticon, technicolored, terricolous, torticollis, toxicogenic, toxicology, toxicosis, tragicomedy, tricolor, tricorn,

tricostate, tricot, tricotine, unicolor, unicorn, unicostate, uricosuric, vari-
colored, varicose, varicotomy, ventricose, versicolor, vidicon, vorticose,
wicopy

#8, "LPH"

Locating six words is fantastic; seven, stupendous; eight, absolutely colossal!

alpha, alphabet, alphanumeric, alphosis, delphinium, dolphin, phenol-
phthalein, ralph, sulphur, sylph, telpher

#9, "EME"

If you find 40, you're a sharpie; 48, you're brilliant; 55, you're a genius!

bereavement, cemetery, cement, cementite, confinement, deme, demeanor,
dementia, demerit, demesne, demeton, emend, emerald, emerge, emergency,
emeritus, emersion, emery, emetic, emeu, ephemeral, excrement, heme, hem-
elytron, hemeralopia, increment, irremeable, irremediable, memento, mince-
meat, misdemeanor, nemertean, nemesis, pavement, phoneme, piecemeal,
premedicate, premeditate, radioelement, rapprochement, redeemer, refine
ment, remedial, remedy, remember, retirement, scheme, seducement, seme,
sememe, semester, siemens, spireme, statement, supplement, supreme, telem-
etry, temerity, theme, tremendous, treponeme, trireme, vehement

WORDWORKS

#1, "Gamester"

(4 letters)
ages, arms, ease, east, game, gate, gear, gems, germ, geta, gram, mare, mart,
mast, mate, meat, meet, mere, mete, rage, rags, rams, rate, ream, rest, sage,
same, sate, seam, sear, seat, seem, seer, sera, sere, seta, stag, star, stem, tame,
tare, tear, team, teem, term, tram, tree

(5 letters)
agree, ameer, aster, eager, eater, egest, egret, ester, gamer, grate, great, mater,
merge, meter, reset, serge, smart, smear, stage, stare, steam, steer, tamer,
tease, terse

(6 letters)
gamest, gamete, grease, master, meager, merest, stream, tamest, teaser

(7 letters)
steamer

#2, "Favorite"

(4 letters)
aver, fair, fare, fate, fear, feat, feta, fiat, fire, five, fore, fort, frat, iota, over, rate, rave, reft, rife, rift, riot, rite, rive, rota, rote, rove, tare, taro, tear, tier, tire, tiro, tore, trio, vert, veto, vote

(5 letters)
afrit, after, avert, favor, forte, irate, orate, ovate, overt, ratio, rivet, trove, voter

#3, "Betrothal"

(4 letters)
abet, able, alto, bale, bare, bate, bath, bear, beat, belt, beta, blat, blot, boar, boat, bola, bolt, bone, bore, both, brat, earl, hale, halo, halt, hart, heal, hear, heat, herb, hero, hoar, hoer, hole, hora, late, lath, lobe, lore, oath, oral, rale, rate, real, robe, role, rota, rote, tale, teal, that, tole, tort, tote, tret, trot

(5 letters)
abhor, abort, alert, alter, bathe, berth, betta, blear, bloat, broth, earth, heart, helot, hotel, labor, later, lathe, loath, obeah, orate, other, otter, table, tabor, taler, tarot, throb, throe, torte, total, treat, troth

(6 letters)
bather, batter, battle, bettor, boater, bolter, bother, bottle, breath, halter, hatter, herbal, hotter, lather, loathe, oblate, rattle, rotate, tablet, threat

(7 letters)
battler, betroth, blather, blotter, bottler, brothel

#4, "Development"

(4 letters)
deem, deep, dele, dent, dole, dolt, dome, done, dope, dote, even, lent, lode, lone, lope, love, meet, meld, melt, mend, mete, mode, mold, mole, molt, mope, mote, move, need, node, nope, note, omen, open, oven, peel, peen, pelt, pend, pent, plod, plot, poem, poet, pole, pond, pone, teem, teen, tend, toed, told, tole, tome, tone, tope, veep, vend, vent, veto, volt, vote

(5 letters)
delve, demon, depot, elope, emote, epode, event, lemon, levee, melon, model, motel, novel, olden, opted, peeve, tempo, tepee, veldt

(6 letters)
deepen, delete, demote, devote, needle, omelet, temple

(7 letters)
deplete, develop, devotee, element

(8 letters)
envelope

(9 letters)
elopement

108

#5, "Exemplary"

(4 letters)
aery, apex, army, axle, earl, eery, exam, lame, lamp, leap, leer, lyre, male, mare, meal, mere, pale, pare, peal, pear, peel, peer, perm, play, plea, pram, pray, prey, rale, ramp, rape, real, ream, reap, reel, rely, yare, year, yelp

(5 letters)
ample, amply, early, emery, expel, layer, leery, leper, maple, mealy, merle, payee, payer, pearl, pryer, realm, relax, relay, repel, reply, xylem

(6 letters)
leaper, merely, parley, pearly, player, replay

(7 letters)
example, lamprey

#6, "Popularity"

(4 letters)
airy, alit, aril, arty, auto, lair, liar, lira, lory, lout, oily, opal, oral, pail, pair, palp, part, pita, pity, plat, play, plop, plot, ploy, port, pour, pray, proa, prop, pulp, pupa, puri, purl, rail, rapt, rial, riot, roil, ropy, rota, roup, rout, tail, tali, taro, tarp, toil, tolu, tori, tour, trap, tray, trio, trip, yaup, your, yurt

(5 letters)
aport, apply, aptly, atrip, laity, lapin, loppy, parol, party, patio, pilot, plait, platy, poilu, polar, polyp, pulpy, pupil, ratio, royal, trail, trial, troup, tulip, ultra

(6 letters)
artily, layout, outlay, papyri, parity, partly, payout, polity, poplar, portal, portly, purity, ripply, uppity

(7 letters)
popular, poultry, topiary

(8 letters)
polarity

#7, "Historical"

(4 letters)
ails, alit, alto, arch, cart, cash, cast, char, chat, chit, clot, coal, coat, coil, cost, hail, hair, halo, hart, hoar, hora, host, iris, itch, laic, lair, lash, last, lath, liar, lira, list, loch, lost, oast, oral, orca, otic, rail, rash, rial, rich, roil rota, sail, salt, sari, scar, scat, shot, silt, slat, slit, slot, soar, soil, sora, sort, star, stir, taco, tail, taro, this, tiro, toil, tola, tori, trio

(5 letters)
actor, ascot, chart, chili, choir, clash, cloth, coast, coral, crash, hoist, latch, loath, loris, ratio, roach, roast, salic, shirt, shoat, short, sloth, stoic, torch, trail, trash, trial, triol

(6 letters)
aortic, castor, choral, racist, sailor, silica, social, starch, thoria, thoric

(7 letters)
chariot, ostrich, trochal

(8 letters)
historic, holistic

#8, "Concentration"

(4 letters)
acne, ante, cane, cant, care, cart, cent, coat, coin, cone, coot, core, corn, cote, earn, icon, into, iota, iron, near, neat, neon, nine, nice, none, noon, note, oleo, olio, once, onto, oral, race, rain, rant, rate, rein, rent, rice, riot, rite, roan, rote, tact, tare, tarn, taro, tart, tear, tent, tier, tine, tint, tire, tone, torn, tort, tote, tret, trot

(5 letters)
actor, antic, atone, attic, cairn, canoe, canon, canto, cater, caret, crane, crate, crone, croon, enact, inate, inert, inner, irate, nonce, octet, onion, orate, otter, ratio, riant, tacit, taint, tarot, tatoo, tenon, titan, toner, tonic, trace, tract, train, trait, trice, trine

(6 letters)
accent, action, arctic, attire, cancer, cannon, cannot, canter, cantor, carton, cornea, cornet, corona, cotton, crater, intact, nation, nectar, notion, octane, ration, retina, rotate, trance

(7 letters)
cartoon, conceit, concern, concert, connect, connote, contact, contain, content, contort, coronet, entrant, nictate, oration, raccoon

(8 letters)
contract, creation, interact, notation, reaction, rotation, traction

(9 letters)
container

(10 letters)
concertina, connection

(11 letters)
contraction

#9, "Xylophone"

(4 letters)
help, hole, holp, holy, hone, hood, hope, hypo, lone, loon, loop, lope, lynx, nope, only, onyx, open, oxen, peon, ploy, pole, polo, pone, pony, pooh, pool

(5 letters)
epoxy, honey, hooey, loony, peony, phlox, phone, phony, pylon

(6 letters)
holpen, openly, phenol, phenyl, phooey

#10, "Nasturtium"

(4 letters)
amir, anti, aunt, main, mart, mash, mast, mina, mint, mist, mitt, must, mutt, nuts, rain, rani, rant, ruin, runt, rust, sari, sima, smut, snit, star, stir, stun, suit, sura, tain, tarn, taut, tint, tram, trim, tsar, tuna, turn, unau, unit, urus

(5 letters)
astir, manus, matin, minus, ramus, riant, saint, satin, sitar, smart, stain, start, stint, stria, strum, strut, stunt, suint, sutra, taint, taunt, train, trait, trust, unarm

(6 letters)
antrum, artist, autism, instar, mantis, martin, mutant, nutria, strain, strait, struma, tanist, truant

(7 letters)
intrust, stratum, transit, uranium

(8 letters)
transmit

#11, "Whispering"

(4 letters)
egis, gens, grew, grin, grip, heir, hers, hewn, hire, news, pens, pews, phew, pier, pine, ping, pins, prig, ring, ripe, rise, sewn, shin, ship, sigh, sign, sine, sing, sire, spew, spin, swig, weir, when, whip, whir, wigs, wine, wing, wipe, wire, wise, wish, wisp

(5 letters)
gripe, hinge, pries, prise, reign, resin, rinse, ripen, risen, shine, shire, shrew, sinew, singe, spine, spire, sprig, swine, swing, weigh, whine, wring

(6 letters)
hewing, hiring, perish, resign, sewing, shiner, shrine, signer, singer, siring, spring, whiner, wiping, wiring

(7 letters)
inspire, swinger, wishing

(9 letters)
perishing

#12, "Politician"

(4 letters)
alit, alto, anil, anti, cant, capo, clan, clap, clip, clop, clot, coal, coat, coil, coin, cola, colt, copt, icon, laic, lain, lint, lion, loan, loin, nail, opal, otic, pact, pail, pant, pica, pint, pion, pita, plan, plat, plot, taco, tail, talc, toil, topi

(5 letters)

actin, aloin, antic, canto, capon, coati, iliac, inapt, ionic, licit, nopal, ontic, optic, paint, panic, patio, piano, picot, pilot, piton, plain, plait, plant, plica, point, talon, tonal, tonic, topic

(6 letters)

action, cation, catnip, italic, oilcan, plaint, pliant, pontil

(7 letters)

capitol, caption, initial, pinitol, politic, topical

PLAYER'S CHOICE

#1

1-G, 2-O, 3-L, 4-X, 5-Q, 6-T, 7-V, 8-H, 9-C, 10-R, 11-I, 12-U, 13-Y, 14-W, 15-S, 16-A, 17-Z, 18-N, 19-F, 20-B, 21-K, 22-M, 23-E, 24-J, 25-P, 26-D

#2

1-R, 2-U, 3-N, 4-Y, 5-K, 6-P, 7-J, 8-E, 9-D, 10-O, 11-A, 12-Q, 13-L, 14-X, 15-B, 16-S, 17-H, 18-C, 19-I, 20-F, 21-W, 22-G, 23-V, 24-M, 25-T

#3

1-S, 2-V, 3-G, 4-A, 5-F, 6-Q, 7-U, 8-X, 9-D, 10-M, 11-H, 12-P, 13-C, 14-W, 15-Z, 16-I, 17-K, 18-O, 19-Y, 20-L, 21-N, 22-E, 23-B, 24-J, 25-R, 26-T

#4

1-M, 2-R, 3-H, 4-P, 5-A, 6-L, 7-U, 8-B, 9-X, 10-Y, 11-Q, 12-V, 13-W, 14-T, 15-F, 16-D, 17-Z, 18-C, 19-G, 20-E, 21-O, 22-N, 23-J, 24-I, 25-K, 26-S

#5

1-N, 2-Q, 3-X, 4-I, 5-R, 6-U, 7-C, 8-K, 9-P, 10-L, 11-A, 12-V, 13-E, 14-T, 15-W, 16-M, 17-Y, 18-D, 19-B, 20-J, 21-H, 22-S, 23-G, 24-O, 25-F

#6

1-O, 2-D, 3-T, 4-K, 5-A, 6-Q, 7-B, 8-F, 9-M, 10-E, 11-S, 12-C, 13-R, 14-J, 15-G, 16-H, 17-N, 18-I, 19-P, 20L

1-I, 2-N, 3-G, 4-E, 5-S, 6-L, 7-B, 8-A, 9-J, 10-Q, 11-C, 12-H, 13-D, 14-F, 15-M, 16-P, 17-T, 18-K, 19-O, 20-R

#8

1-W, 2-I, 3-R, 4-C, 5-H, 6-U, 7-L, 8-Y, 9-N, 10-A, 11-Q, 12-K, 13-V, 14-D, 15-G, 16-M, 17-S, 18-X, 19-J, 20-B, 21-P, 22-F, 23-T, 24-O, 25-E

#9

1-O, 2-T, 3-W, 4-P, 5-K, 6-S, 7-N, 8-Q, 9-B, 10-V, 11-F, 12-R, 13-E, 14-U, 15-Y, 16-H, 17-C, 18-I, 19-X, 20-A, 21-D, 22-J, 23-M, 24-G, 25-L

#10

1-K, 2-O, 3-A, 4-V, 5-I, 6-R, 7-N, 8-T, 9-W, 10-Q, 11-S, 12-C, 13-X, 14-U, 15-D, 16-M, 17-J, 18-F, 19-P, 20-Y, 21-G, 22-B, 23-L, 24-E, 25-H

LETTER PERFECT

#1

1. Tournament, 2. Teapot, 3. Transcript, 4. Tot, 5. Telecast, 6. Tut, 7. Tempest, 8. Truculent, 9. Translucent, 10. Text, 11. Testament, 12. Tantamount, 13. Trumpet, 14. Thermostat, 15. Tenderfoot, 16. Thirst, 17. Tat, 18. Tonight, 19. Tact, 20. Tryst

#2

1. Transparent, 2. Tenement, 3. Turnabout, 4. Treat, 5. Tart, 6. Tenet, 7. Tacit, 8. Triplet, 9. Temperament, 10. Turncoat, 11. Tangent, 12. Transplant, 13. Turret, 14. Transient, 15. Tablet, 16. Truant, 17. Tourist, 18. Threat, 19. Taut, 20. Tent, 21. Trout

#3

1. Earthenware, 2. Edifice, 3. Ensemble, 4. Evacuate, 5. Engrave, 6. Earthquake, 7. Eloquence, 8. Embezzle, 9. Enumerate, 10. Evidence, 11. Esplanade, 12. Exorcise, 13. Equate, 14. Eave, 15. Elapse, 16. Escape, 17. Excuse, 18. Elegance, 19. Epicure, 20. Encourage, 21. Espadrille, 22. Effervescence, 23. Educate, 24. Editorialize, 25. Elaborate

#4

1. Exaggerate, 2. Eye, 3. Entire, 4. Employee, 5. Endure, 6. Eke, 7. Exuberance, 8. Embrace, 9. Eliminate, 10. Explode, 11. Eerie, 12. Estate, 13. Entrance, 14. Expatriate, 15. Enclave, 16. Expensive, 17. Electorate, 18. Enforce, 19. Envelope, 20. Equine, 21. Ease, 22. Enterprise, 23. Esquire, 24. Elude, 25. Eagle, 26. Ebbtide, 27. Exile, 28. Epilogue, 29. Ermine, 30. Eligible

#5

1. Liverpool, 2. Landfill, 3. Laurel, 4. Lysol, 5. Libel, 6. Lateral, 7. Lentil, 8. Logroll, 9. Label, 10. Liberal, 11. Lull, 12. Literal, 13. Lil, 14. Loyal, 15. Lethal, 16. Loll, 17. Lackadaisical, 18. Lapel, 19. Lyrical, 20. Local, 21. Logical

#6

1. Nightgown, 2. Noggin, 3. Nonagon, 4. Nylon, 5. Nobleman, 6. Newton, 7. Neon, 8. Nitrogen, 9. Napkin, 10. Newman, 11. Notion, 12. Nubbin, 13. Noon, 14. Nation, 15. Nineteen, 16. Nixon, 17. Napoleon, 18. Nolan, 19. Newborn, 20. Nun, 21. Nelson, 22. Neutron, 23. Nickelodeon, 24. Nucleon

#7

1. Haunch, 2. Horseradish, 3. High, 4. Hopscotch, 5. Hooch, 6. Hash, 7. Hogwash, 8. Howdah, 9. Hyacinth, 10. Hallelujah, 11. Hearth, 12. Hairsbreadth, 13. Halvah, 14. Hannah, 15. Hush, 16. Harrah, 17. Homograph, 18. Henceforth, 19. Hunch, 20. Hurrah, 21. Hugh, 22. Homestretch, 23. Health, 24. Hitch, 25. Hashish, 26. Hutch

#8

1. Raconteur, 2. Receiver, 3. Rumor, 4. Rooster, 5. Rigor, 6. Rustler, 7. River, 8. Radiator, 9. Reindeer, 10. Rear, 11. Roar, 12. Ranger, 13. Redeemer, 14. Revolver, 15. Renoir, 16. Ruler, 17. Rancor, 18. Rathskeller, 19. Rudder, 20. Rambler, 21. Rather, 22. Rapier, 23. Recur, 24. Recover, 25. Render, 26. Radar, 27. Regular

#9

1. Deceased, 2. Dachshund, 3. David, 4. Dilapidated, 5. Diamond, 6. Doodad, 7. Dryad, 8. Distend, 9. Devoid, 10. Dread, 11. Disregard,

12. Dividend, 13. Dagwood, 14. Dashboard, 15. Disneyland, 16. Dud, 17. Dead, 18. Deformed, 19. Dollywood, 20. Dad, 21. Descend, 22. Deed, 23. Discord, 24. Dastard, 25. Druid, 26. Demigod

#10

1. Sacrilegious, 2. Spontaneous, 3. Spyglass, 4. Sophocles, 5. Stylus, 6. Suppress, 7. Superfluous, 8. Sans, 9. Sedulous, 10. Stress, 11. Symbiosis, 12. Stradivarius, 13. Sweepstakes, 14. Studious, 15. Sinus, 16. Scandalous, 17. Synopsis, 18. Slanderous, 19. Swiss, 20. Spineless, 21. Surreptitious

GREAT BEGINNINGS

#1

1. Incentive, 2. Incognito, 3. Infallible, 4. Inn, 5. Invoice, 6. Intrepid, 7. Interloper, 8. Insomnia, 9. Inherit, 10. Inmate, 11. Infirmity, 12. Inch, 13. Injure, 14. Inert, 15. Interrogate, 16. Infant, 17. Incubate, 18. Inferno, 19. Indigo, 20. Indiana, 21. Infantry, 22. Indict, 23. Ink

#2

1. Expel, 2. Exit, 3. Exempt, 4. Excellent, 5. Exaggerate, 6. Extra, 7. Exam, 8. Experiment, 9. Expression, 10. Excuse, 11. Exodus, 12. Expensive, 13. Exile, 14. Exact, 15. Excalibur, 16. Extraterrestrial, 17. Expand, 18. Exhaustion, 19. Expressway, 20. Executioner, 21, Export, 22. Extrovert

#3

1. Quagmire, 2. Quartet, 3. Quilt, 4. Quack, 5. Quake, 6. Quiet, 7. Quarrel, 8. Quicksand, 9. Queen, 10. Quandary, 11. Quaker, 12. Quarantine, 13. Quail, 14. Quarry, 15. Quisling, 16. Quaff, 17. Quirk, 18. Query, 19. Queue, 20. Quaint, 21. Quell, 22. Quinine, 23. Quince, 24. Quarterback, 25. Quip

#4

1. Wacky, 2. Wafer, 3. Waldorf salad, 4. Waft, 5. Waitress, 6. Wagon, 7. Waif, 8. Walrus, 9. Wallaby, 10. Walnut, 11. Wanton, 12. Wallflower,

13. Wax, 14. Wattle, 15. Wardrobe, 16. Washboard, 17. Warble, 18. War-path, 19. Washington, 20. Warlock, 21. Wanderlust, 22. Waltz

#5

1. Shadow, 2. Sherbet, 3. Shakespeare, 4. Shallot, 5. Shyster, 6. Shard, 7. Shroud, 8. Shirk, 9. Shrapnel, 10. Sham, 11. Shrine, 12. Shilling, 13. Shrug, 14. Sheriff, 15. Shrub, 16. Sheaf, 17. Shoat, 18. Shortening, 19. Shriek, 20. Shrimp, 21. Shrew, 22. Shun

#6

1. Poetry, 2. Porcelain, 3. Poltergeist, 4. Polygraph, 5. Poach, 6. Poi, 7. Pontiff, 8. Portfolio, 9. Pollen, 10. Porcupine, 11. Portrait, 12. Posture, 13. Poker, 14. Poppycock, 15. Pompadour, 16. Polka, 17. Posse, 18. Polaris, 19. Politburo, 20. Pony Express

#7

1. Mandate, 2. Marmoset, 3. Madrigal, 4. Marble, 5. Martian, 6. Major-domo, 7. Martyr, 8. Macaroni, 9. Mardi Gras, 10. Maneuver, 11. Maze, 12. Malaria, 13. Marsh, 14. Macbeth, 15. Marathon, 16. Manicure, 17. Mambo, 18. Martini, 19. Magenta

#8

1. Foal, 2. Folly, 3. Forte, 4. Fondue, 5. Forgery, 6. Football, 7. Foe, 8. Footnote, 9. Forever, 10. Font, 11. Foliage, 12. Forest, 13. Forceps, 14. Foible, 15. Fodder, 16. Fob, 17. Forage, 18. Foundling, 19. Fortnight, 20. Fossil, 21. Forget-me-not, 22. Forbid

#9

1. Noodle, 2. Nostalgia, 3. November, 4. Notch, 5. Noah, 6. Nominee, 7. Noxious, 8. Nonchalant, 9. Noise, 10. Novena, 11. Noel, 12. Nobel (Alfred), 13. Noose, 14. Nozzle, 15. Nom de plume, 16. Notary, 17. Nougat, 18. Note, 19. Nomad, 20. Nocturnal, 21. Novice, 22. North Pole, 23. Nodule

#10

1. Trace, 2. Trellis, 3. Trophy, 4. Tribe, 5. Tragedy, 6. Transom, 7. Troglodyte, 8. Trampoline, 9. Tranquil, 10. Triumph, 11. Trousseau, 12. Trawl, 13. Trapeze, 14. Truffle, 15. Transcend, 16. Triad, 17. Trauma, 18. Trifle, 19. Trowel

WORD CHASE

#1

```
D A F F O D I L I U Q N O J
O I O E X R R E D N A E L O
G L R Y P U C R E T T U B H
W O S N A P D R A G O N E N
O N Y O N S E S U E T S T N
O G T E S K I T M Y O T O Y
D A H P Y R K O U R P O N J
A M I P I A E A Z N G P Y U
S E A H O L L Y N I I X O M
T I L L C A S A G E N A T P
E G I O G I D N I P B N R II
R L L X A I L H A D O R I P
Y A Y D O H Y D R A N G E A
C H R Y S A N T H E M U M V
```

#2

```
W E I M A R A N E R G O D I
H Y N A I T A M L A D E A N
I K A T O X F F I T S A M U
P S F N S A L U K I Z L Y L
P U G I A P N L R K H V N A
E H H A Z I B F C A C I A S
T N A S H E N A S W A Z T C
E A N C A O F A S P I S T H
R I O G H C A I R E R L I N
R R L C O P L E M E N A R A
I E I R S K I L U P M J B U
E B G O Y A X B O R Z O I Z
R I O D N U O H Y E R G P P
E S E G N I K E P B O X E R
```

#3

```
A B Y S S I N I A N S O M E
R H U C I L A M O S H I N S
O A A R A G D O L L O T C E
G V M O M A N X A I R O D N
N A N C E E D A B A T N E L
H A I S I S I M T H K V L
A I C E C R E I B A I O A
S B T A T M O S Z O I N N B
I R P T A P H O M B R E R O
K O Y N R F E A N A I S E C
R W G C O R N I S H R E X A
U N E L K D O P Y A B M O B
T A D E U L B N A I S S U R
```

#4

```
S D U O L C T N A R G A R F
L N U I L L A D E M D U E T
O F O X Y L A D Y P I C L H
V S O W A Y D U G I T I D G
E U M A B E I A C N E N O I
L N Q O V R R D E K A D O N
L F U I N N I N X F N E D K
O L L A E C I D D A W R E T
D A X T Y M H O E V A E E E
A R T P O A N E N O D L K L
N E P R I J A D R R W L N R
I A P L U V V I E L E A A A
H C E A E U G I R T N I Y C
C O N F I D E N C E O L E S
```

#5

```
N I T R A M E C H A P L I N
O E G A R R E L D I M A P O
T P B R O O K S W E S T O M
L O Y O L S R E L L E S W M
E H M X R A M U R P H Y E E
K W L M A T T H A U R L L
S I L K I T X A W F M C L D
D L A E O N E N Y O A O E R
L L F B L E O A S N Y S N E
E I B L A L D T H D N T O Y
I A U B E L I N A A H E T F
F M O E A A L A N E A L A U
A S K O O R B R K E K L E S
W I L D E R I G S T X O K S
```

#6

```
A Y E F A H L O M B A R D I
A L N O S K C A J E N A Y R
R A E X U N I L S O G Z O N
O L O X C Y R E S I E R Z E
N L I O A E C N A H G U A V
O E G S M N I M C C O V E Y
S N G L A B D R E K A E P S
N A A V O E X E T Y W F C A
I P M R A A Z T R E H H O Y
B M I N F I E R R S M A B R
O A D U M R I A U I H T U R
R C O B B C C O D G R O V E
I K S M E Z R T S A Y O T T
```

#7

```
L A N G E K U D E N N I S N
E M A H A R G R E T N U H E
A L E I N A D C M H O L M G
C L E M O S C A R A S T O R
H E R O D I M E R W O N K U
M W E R R R S X O N O T E B
A R V E O X O T V T N H D N
N A E N G E R F E A U T R E
A D R O A R S L R N M I O E
M S T R E E P G T E O M V T
G E O T N A R G X M H S A S
R Y X O T F A B A I N T E R
E A J S H U S T O N L L U H
B H M C C A M B R I D G E R
```

#8

```
M A S L A B A G I E L G U D
A F N N U D S V I W I N S D
T N I O X D E N I R O U C O
T R C T I S T O R S X O H U
H U H S Z N O T T U H Y I G
A B O U M G S R I S B C L L
U O L H I A E C D H P X D A
S C S A L B P R R E O Y K S
T E O V L E A I A F E E R N
I H N A S B U S O L A R A O
N C D L O U Q P G I D G U T
O E F R A G W E N N O X T T
V M S N R U B R E N N A N U
W A L K E N A M E S U O H B
```

STIR CRAZIES

#1

Peach, Grape, Orange, Tomato, Watermelon, Cantaloupe, Pineapple, Cherry

#2

Tan slacks, Pink shirt, Brown shoes, Argyle socks, Blue blazer, Paisley tie, Maroon vest, Leather belt

#3

The Stand, The Dead Zone, Christine, Firestarter, The Dark Tower, Pet Sematary, Salem's Lot, The Shining

#4

Body Heat, Sweet Dreams, The Accused, Rain Man, Atlantic City, Wall Street, The Verdict, Die Hard

#5

Nancy Drew, Nora Charles, Nero Wolfe, Miss Marple, Charlie Chan, Sam Spade, Nick Charles, Hercule Poirot

#6

Banyan, Mahogany, Redwood, Poplar, Magnolia, Sycamore, Chinaberry, Persimmon

#7

Cardinal, Sparrow, Sandpiper, Swallow, Partridge, Pigeon, Woodpecker, Sapsucker

#8

Saxophone, Glockenspiel, Mandolin, Concertina, Accordion, Harmonica, Trombone, Triangle

#9

Peach bombe, Charlotte russe, Lemon souffle, Orange sorbet, Apricot mousse, Bread pudding, Peach melba, Caramel parfait

#10

William Styron, William Faulkner, Eudora Welty, Alice Walker, James Thurber, Stephen Crane, Ernest Hemingway, Margaret Mitchell

STORY BUILDERS

#1

it, sit, pits, trips, priest, respite

#2

be, bet, debt, bated, debate, berated

#3

pa, apt, rapt, prate, tamper, primate

#4

do, sod, does, posed, despot, spotted

#5

no, one, peon, prone, person, ponders, responds

at, art, rant, train, retain, certain, reaction, creations

pa, pal, pale, pleas, asleep, repeals, prelates

a, as, sea, eras, tears, traces, creates, as secret

or, row, word, drown, wonder, downers, worsened

per, reap, pearl, parley, reapply

SAY IT AGAIN, SAM

#1

compliment, acclaim, praise, laud, commend

#2

effort, endeavor, attempt, strive, try

#3

adversary, rival, antagonist, enemy, predator

#4

instruct, train, teach, educate, tutor

#5

secret, enigma, mystery, riddle, puzzle

#6

eject, evict, exclude, expel, oust

#7

garbage, waste, trash, rubbish, refuse

121

#8

consider, cogitate, deliberate, ruminate, ponder

#9

mistake, omission, fallacy, blunder, error

#10

implore, entreat, beseech, appeal, plead

TAKE FIVE

#1

	S	C	O	R	E
AMERICAN INDIANS	Seneca Shoshone Sioux	Cherokee Comanche Crow	Ojibway Osage	Ree Rikari	Erie
ICE CREAM FLAVORS	Strawberry	Chocolate	Orange	Raspberry Rocky Road	Eggnog
BIBLICAL FIGURES	Salome Saul Solomon	Cain Christ	Obadiah Ozymandius	Rachel Raphael Ruth	Esther Ezekiel
VEGETABLES	Spinach Squash	Cabbage Cauliflower Corn	Okra Onion	Radish Rutabaga	Eggplant Endive
COLORS	Scarlet Sienna	Cerulean Coral Crimson	Ochre Olive	Red Russet	Ebony Ecru

#2

	R	G	P	S	B
CHEESES	Romano Roquefort	Gorgonzola Gouda	Parmesan Provolone	Saanen Swiss	Boursin Brie
FEMALE SINGERS	Helen Reddy	Crystal Gayle	Patti Page Dolly Parton	Carly Simon	Joan Baez Anita Baker

Linda Ronstadt Diana Ross	Lesley Gore		Grace Slick Barbra Streisand	Pat Benatar
BODIES OF WATER	Red Lake Red Sea	Guanabara Bay Gulf of Mexico	Pacific Ocean Persian Gulf	Salton Sea Sea of Cortez Strait of Magellan	Baltic Sea Bering Sea Black Sea
MEN'S FIRST NAMES	Ralph Richard Robert Roger	George Gilbert Grant	Paul Perry Peter Philip	Sal Simon Steve Stuart	Bill Bruce Bryan
CARD GAMES	Red Dog Rummy Russian Bank	Garbage Gin Go Fish	Parliament Pinochle Poker	Sixty-Six Skat Solitare	Baccarat Blackjack Bridge

#3

	D	**A**	**B**	**S**	**P**
STATE CAPITALS	Denver Des Moines Dover	Albany Austin Atlanta	Baton Rouge Bismarck Boise	Sacramento Salem Salt Lake City	Phoenix Pierre Providence
CARTOON CHAR- ACTERS	Daffy Duck Donald Duck Dudley Doright	Archie Atom Ant	Betty Boop Bugs Bunny Bullwinkle	Scooby Doo Spiderman Superman	Pepe Le Pew Popeye Porky Pig
TELEVISION SOAP OPERAS	Dallas Days of Our Lives Dynasty	All My Children As The World Turns	(The) Bold and The Beautiful	Santa Barbara Search For Tomorrow	Peyton Place
PROFESSIONS	Dancer Dentist Doctor Draftsman	Actor Astronaut Auctioneer Author	Baker Barber Bartender Butler	Salesclerk Scribe Shepherd Surgeon	Policeman Potter Preacher
CARY GRANT MOVIES	Destination Tokyo Dream Wife	(The) Awful Truth An Affair to Re- member	(The) Bishop's Wife Bringing Up Baby	Suspicion Sylvia Scarlett	Penny Serenade Philadelphia Story

123

	C	H	A	M	P
MOVIE TITLES	Casablanca (The) Color Purple Cool Hand Luke	Harold and Maude High Noon (The) Hustler	Adam's Rib All About Eve Annie Hall	Marnie Married to the Mob Marty Moonstruck	Parenthood Pinocchio (The) Producers
NUTS	Cashew Castana Chestnut	Hazel Head Hickory	Acorn Almond Applenut	Macadamia Maranon Mast	Peanut Pecan Pistachio
TREES	Carob Cedar Chinaberry	Hardtack Haw Hickory	Alder Ash Aspen	Maple Mimosa Mulberry	Pecan Pine Poplar
7-LETTER NOUNS	Clothes Coaster Command Culvert	Handful Heathen History Hygiene	Admiral Alimony Ammonia Avarice	Mammoth Mineral Mongrel Monster	Pattern Playpen Poultry Primary
PRO FOOTBALL PLAYERS	Earl Campbell Dwight Clark	Drew Hill Tony Hill Paul Hornung	Troy Aikman Marcus Allen Lyle Alzado	Dan Marino Joe Montana Jim McMahon	Drew Pearson Dan Pastorini

	W	S	C	B	R
PROFES-SIONAL GOLFERS	Tom Watson Tom Weiskopf	Gene Sarazen Sam Snead Curtis Strange	Billy Casper Bruce Crampton	Seve Bal-lesteros Julius Boros	Mike Reid Chi Chi Rodriguez
SEAFOOD	Walleye Whitefish	Salmon Scrod Sole	Catfish Cod Crayfish	Bass Bluefish Butterfish	Red Snapper Roughy
TELEVISION NEWS-CASTERS	Mike Wallace Barbara Walters	Morley Safer Diane Sawyer Bernard Shaw	Connie Chung Walter Cronkite	Ed Bradley David Brinkley Tom Brokaw	Dan Rather Harry Reasoner
BROADWAY MUSICALS	West Side Story Wildcat	Show Boat South Pacific	Cabaret Cats (A) Chorus Line	Band Wagon Brigadoon Bye Bye Birdie	Rhapsody Rumple

WORLD CAPITALS	Warsaw Washington, D.C.	San Salvador Santiago Sydney Singapore	Cairo Caracas Copenhagen	Brasilia Brussels Bucharest Budapest	Reykjavik Rome

#6

	T	S	M	R	C
TELEVISION SLEUTHS	Dan Tanna Vinnie Terranova Harry S. Truman	Maxwell Smart Remington Steele B. L. Stryker	Thomas Magnum Mannix McCloud	Rockford	Cannon Columbo Dale Cooper
FAIRY TALES	Three Little Pigs	Snow White and the Seven Dwarfs	Mother Goose	Rapunzel	Cinderella
CHILD STARS	Elizabeth Taylor Shirley Temple	Fred Savage Ricky Schroeder Brooke Shields	Jerry Mathers Hayley Mills	Mickey Rooney Kurt Russell	Kirk Cameron Jackie Coogan
DANCES	Tango Twist	Samba Square Dance Swim	Mambo Mashed Potato Monkey	Reel Rumba	Cancan Cha-Cha Charleston Conga
MODES OF TRAVEL	Taxi Train Tricycle Trolley car	Skateboard Space Shuttle Subway	Moped Motorcycle	Raft Rickshaw Rocket ship Rowboat	Canoe Car Caravan Carriage

#7

	G	R	E	A	T
MOVIE STARS	Clark Gable Greta Garbo Cary Grant	Robert Redford Christopher Reeve	Emilio Estevez Dame Edith Evans Tom Ewell	Alan Alda Julie Andrews Dan Akroyd	Rip Torn Spencer Tracy Kathleen Turner
FLOWERS	Gardenia Geranium Gladiolus	Rhodora Rose	Edelweiss Elite Essence	Amaryllis Aster Azalea	Truss Tulip Tutty
CAR/TRUCK MODELS	Grand Prix Gremlin Grenada	Ram Ranchero Regal	Eagle Edsel Excel	Accord Ambassador Aries	Taurus Torino Toronado

125

FOREIGN COUNTRIES	Germany	Romania	Egypt	Albania	Taiwan
	Great Britain	Russia	El Salvador	Algeria	Tunisia
	Greenland	Rwanda	Ethiopia	Argentina	Turkey
RIVERS	Ganges	Rhine	Ebola	Allegheny	Thames
	Gila	Rhone	Elbe	Arkansas	Tiber
	Green	Rio Grande	Euphrates	Avon	Truckee

#8

	C	M	O	G	S
SPORTS-CASTERS	Harry Carey	John Madden	Pat O'Brien	Joe Garagiola	O J Simpson
	Bob Costas	Jim McKay		Frank Gifford	Dick Stockton
		Al Michaels		Greg Gumbel	Pat Summerall
		Brent Musberger			
MIXED DRINKS	Cape Cod	Mai Tai	Orange Fizz	Gimlet	Sloe Gin Fizz
	Cuba libra	Manhattan		Gin & Tonic	Screwdriver
		Martini			
		Mimosa			
BIRDS	Canary	Meadowlark	Oriole	Goldfinch	Sandpiper
	Cardinal	Mockingbird	Osprey	Goose	Sparrow
	Chickadee	Mynah	Ostrich	Grebe	Starling
	Crow		Owl	Grouse	Swallow
MINERALS	Cinnabar	Malachite	Oroide	Gold	Silica
	Copper	Mica	Orthoclase	Graphite	Sulfur
	Corundum	Microline		Gypsum	
	Cryolite				
CANDY BRANDS	Cadbury's	Mars Bar	O Henry	Good & Plenty	Snickers
	Carmella	Milk Duds		Goo Goo Cluster	Sugar Babies
	Charleston Chew	Mr. Goodbar			
	Cherry Mash				

#9

	M	A	D	E	N
PAST OR PRESENT WORLD LEADERS	Meir	Adenauer	De Gaulle	Eben	Nehru
	Mubarak	Attlee	De Valera	Eisenhower	Nixon
	Mulroney				Noriega
	Mussolini				

INVENTORS	Samuel Morse	Nicholas Appert	John Deere	George Eastman	Alfred Nobel
	Guglielmo Marconi	Howard Aiken	Leonardo Da Vinci	Thomas Edison	Thomas Newcomen
MAMMALS	Marmoset	Aardvark	Deer	Eland	Narwhal
	Mongoose	Anteater	Dik Dik	Elephant	Numbat
	Monkey	Antelope	Dog	Elk	
ELVIS PRESLEY SONGS	Make Me Know It	Are You Lonesome Tonight	Don't Be Cruel	Easy Come, Easy Go	Night Rider
		All Shook Up	Devil In Disguise	End of the Road	
			Don't		
OPERAS	Madam Butterfly	Aida	Don Carlos	Elektra	Nabucco
	(The) Marriage of Figaro	Alcina	Don Giovanni	Eugene Onegin	Norma
		Andrea Chenier			(The) Nose

#10

	G	E	C	A	S
HERBS	Garlic	Elder	Chervil	Alecost	Saffron
	Gentian	Eryngium	Chicory	Angelica	Sage
			Cumin		
US ASTRO-NAUTS	John Glenn	Donn Eisele	Scott Carpenter	Buzz Aldrin	Walter Schirra
	Virgil Grissom	Anthony England	Michael Collins	Neil Armstrong	Alan Shepard
MAGAZINES	GQ	Ebony	Cook's	Advertising Age	Southern Living
	Glamour	Elle	Country Living	Architectural Digest	Sports Illustrated
	Gourmet	Esquire	Car & Driver	Auto Age	Spy
FRUITS	Grape	Elderberry	Cherry	Apple	Strawberry
	Grapefruit		Coconut	Apricot	
	Guava		Cranberry		
			Currant		
POETS	Kahlil Gibran	T S Eliot	Samuel Coleridge	Conrad Aiken	Carl Sandburg
	Thomas Gray	Ralph Waldo Emerson	e.e. cummings	W H Auden	Sir Walter Scott
	Robert Graves				

INDEX

Pages shown in boldface contain the answers.